Executive Documents
2d S 16th Congress
Library
House of Representatives
Doc. 10

LETTER
FROM
THE COMPTROLLER OF THE TREASURY,
TRANSMITTING
A LIST OF BALANCES

On the Books of the Second and Third Auditors of the Treasury, Which Have Remained Due More Than Three Years Prior to the 30th September, 1820; a List of the Names of Persons Who Have Failed to Render Their Accounts to the Said Auditors within the Year; and a List of Advances Made Prior to 3d March, 1809, by the War Department, Which Remained to Be Accounted for on the Books of the Third Auditor of the Treasury on 30th September, 1820

Prepared for the National Society United States Daughters of 1812
by
LTC Linda L. Green, Librarian National

HERITAGE BOOKS
2016

HERITAGE BOOKS

AN IMPRINT OF HERITAGE BOOKS, INC.

Books, CDs, and more—Worldwide

For our listing of thousands of titles see our website
at
www.HeritageBooks.com

Published 2016 by
HERITAGE BOOKS, INC.
Publishing Division
5810 Ruatan Street
Berwyn Heights, Md. 20740

Prepared for the National Society United States Daughters of 1812
by LTC Linda L. Green, Librarian National

* * * * *
November 27, 1820
Ordered to lie on the table

Washington:
Originally Printed by Gales & Seaton
1820

Reprinted by Permission
Granted July 10, 2007
by
Mr. Michael Harrison
House Administration Committee
* * * * *

International Standard Book Numbers
Paperbound: 978-0-7884-5714-2
Clothbound: 978-0-7884-6426-3

TREASURY DEPARTMENT,

COMPTROLLER'S OFFICE
27TH NOVEMBER, 1820.

Sir: In compliance with the provisions of the act of Congress, passed on the 3d March, 1809, entitled "An act further to amend the several acts for the establishment and regulation of the Treasury, War and Navy Departments," and the act, passed on 3d March 1817, entitled "An act to provide for the prompt settlement of public accounts," I have the honor to transmit, herewith, the following returns, received from the Second and Third Auditors of the Treasury, viz:

1. A list of the accounts which have remained unsettled, or on which balances Appear to have been due more than three years, prior to 30th September, 1820, extracted from the books of the Second Auditor of the Treasury.
2. A similar list, extracted from the books of the Third Auditor of the Treasury.
3. A list of those persons who have failed to render their accounts within the year to the Second Auditor of the Treasury for settlement.
4. A similar list rendered by the Third Auditor of the Treasury, including the balances unaccounted for, advanced one year prior to the 30th September, 1819.
5. A list of moneys advanced prior to the 3d March, 1809, on the books of the late Accountant of the War Department, and which remained to be accounted for on the books of the Third Auditor of the Treasury on the 30th September, 1820.

I also transmit, herewith, a letter from the Third Auditor of the Treasury, which accompanies his returns.

With great respect,
I have the honor to be,
Your obedient servant,
Joseph Anderson
Comptroller.

The Hon. John W. Taylor,
Speaker of the House of Representatives.

Sir: In presenting the annual "statement of accounts, in the office of the Third Auditor, which have remained unsettled, or on which balances appear to have been due more than three years," as directed by law, it may be proper to offer some remarks as to the magnitude of the amount, as well as to the number of accounts, which appear to be unsettled in the office. It will be recollected, that, on the 29th of April, 1816, an act passed authorizing appointment of an additional Accountant to the War Department, whose duty it was "to adjust and settle all the accounts in that Department, existing at the conclusion of the late war, and were then unsettled;" including, consequently, every unsettled account in the War Department, from the commencement of the present government, to the 1st of July, 1815, the period fixed upon, as that to which his settlements should extend. This office succeeded by that of the Third Auditor of the Treasury, on the 3d of March, 1817, with the additional duties attached, of auditing the following accounts of the War Department, viz. The accounts for subsisting the army, including those of contractors, storekeepers, and issuing commissaries. The accounts of the quartermaster department, both as to month and public property. The accounts for fortifications of ports and harbors. The accounts for payments to invalid, and revolutionary, and half-pay pensioners. "And, generally, such other accounts of the War Department as were not specifically provided for." At the commencement of the duties of the additional Accountant, on the 8th Ma--, 1816, the outstanding and unsettled accounts amounted to more than forty three millions of dollars, distributed in the hands of several thousand persons, constituting every denomination of disbursing officers, in every department of the army.

Such of the accounts as had been rendered, remained in the offices of the Accountant of the War Department, and Paymaster General, unsettled. These, on being transferred to this office, were found to be defective in a variety of particulars; in many cases no accounts had been rendered for the money advanced; in others they had been rendered only in part; and, in almost all cases, explanations and additional vouchers were necessary, before settlements could be made.

It was also found, that many of the debtors who had received public money from the principal disbursing officers, whose accounts remained unsettled, had not consequently been charged on the books; and it therefore became necessary, in the first place, to investigate all the accounts, to ascertain who had received the public money, and whether the individuals by whom it was to be disbursed had rendered their accounts; for, to have awaited the regular settlement of each account, to ascertain these points, it would have left, even to this time, many persons uncalled upon for their accounts, and the settlements made would have been uncertain, as to their accuracy.

In this state of the business, it became necessary to open a correspondence with every receiver of public money. Volumes have been filled with such letters, and by these and other means a most successful result was produced, in bringing forward numerous accounts for settlement that had not before been rendered. Since that period, settlements have progressed as rapidly as the nature of the accounts would admit, and they have resulted in reducing the outstanding accounts and balanced to the amount stated.

Of this amount it may also be observed, that many of the accounts have been examined, and remain unsettled for want of additional vouchers and explanations, which have been called for; others require but a short time to complete, and several of the balances have been reduced since the statement was commenced. But, independent of the labors consequent to the settlement of such immense accounts of long standing, other duties have required attention, and which have interfered with their settlement. When this office was established, a number of paymasters and other agents were in service for the purpose of paying off the outstanding claims during the late war, in every part of the county.

These officers were speedily discharged, and the outstanding claims ordered to be sent to this office for settlement, and they have been settled to the number of several thousands. Other accounts, also, (unconnected with the balances outstanding,) to a large amount, and extremely voluminous, have been examined in this office, of which number, those of the several states, for disbursements during the late war, may be mentioned: much time and labor is also consequent to an arrangement which requires the Auditor to conduct all the correspondence in relation to every account received in the office, some idea of the extent of which may be formed, when it is stated that, since the establishment of the office, twenty-three letter books have been filled with the letters written on the business of the office.

Some delay in the settlement of the outstanding accounts has also arisen, from the necessity of employing several of the clerks allowed during the last session of Congress for settling them, in preparing statements of the number of militia in service during the late war, and other information, in obedience to resolutions of the Senate and House of Representatives of the last session, a business from the manner in which the militia were paid by the several paymasters and states, requiring a great length of time to complete.

Such are some of the particularizes of the duties devolved on the office of the Third Auditor, and of the employment of the force heretofore allotted to it; this force will, by law, be diminished at the end of the present year, in the discharge of nine clerks; it is, nevertheless, anticipated, that, with a diligent application of the remainder of it, independent of the current business of the office, great progress will be made in reducing the number of the unsettled accounts.

I have the honor to be

Your most obedient servant,

PETER HANGER, Auditor

JOSEPH ANDERSON, Esq.
    First Comptroller of the Treasury

National Society United States Daughters of 1812
1461 Rhode Island Avenue, N.W.
Washington, D. C.

This manuscript was prepared for the National Society United States Daughters of 1812 by LTC Linda L. Green, Librarian National. The manuscript is identical to the original publication except that the original publication used fold-out pages which made the book larger in thickness but fewer in pages with smaller print. As the original was published in 1820, some of the pages had become much worn or were torn/split at the fold. This was unfortunate because the splits were in the dollars/cents column. There are notes as to how this was handled on those pages affected. The pages were near the end of the original publication. The original publication is being maintained by Mrs. Charlotte Young Slinkard Past President National.

LTC Linda L. Green
Librarian National 2006-2009

No. 1

STATEMENT of Accounts, which have remained unsettled, or on which Balances appear to have been due, more than three years, prior to the 30th September, 1820, as appears from the Books of the Second Auditor of the Treasury: furnished in pursuance of the second section of the act of Congress, passed the 3d March, 1809, entitled "An act further to amend the several acts for the establishment and regulation of the Treasury War, and Navy, Departments."

Names and Rank	Amount Dolls.Cts.	Remarks
John Hutchinson, contractor	1,375.23	Reported to the First Comptroller of the Treasury, for suit, 20th May, 1817.
Richard Bland Lee, late superintendent of claims	500.00	Ditto ditto 1st May, 1820.
Joseph Shomo, lieutenant 4th infantry	540.38	Called upon, repeatedly, without effect.
George Jones, chairman of commissioners Savannah	1,000.00	Dead. No information can be obtained respecting the amount.
Thomas W. Denton, lieutenant	824.00	Reported to the First Comptroller of the Treasury, for suit, 15th August, 1820.
Richard H. Bell, captain 7th infantry	800.00	Ditto ditto 29th April, 1818.
William Christy, late paymaster	9,000.00	Ditto ditto 5th December, 1816.
Charles Tyler, late contractor	1,345.83	Ditto ditto 24th June, 1819.
John Conrad, late paymaster of militia	75.00	Ditto ditto 30th September, 1819.
John Byers, late contractor	6,240.48	Ditto ditto 6th February, 1818.
James Gigniliat, lieutenant of artillery	100.00	Ditto ditto 30th September, 1819.
David Riddle, brevet major	430.00	Called upon, repeatedly, without effect.
Adrien Niel, late captain	182.88	Dead.
James P. B. Romayne, late captain of artillery	375.00	Dead.
Hugh Young, assistant topographical engineer	745.82	Accounts in the office of the Third Auditor, but not sufficient to cover the charges against him.
Samuel Y. Balch, late lieutenant 24th infantry	36.00	Out of service. Place of residence unknown.
Jacob Whistler, late lieutenant 1st infantry	102.00	Ditto ditto
William I. Gordon, lieutenant rifle regiment	30.00	Resigned, without settling his accounts, Place of residence unknown.
R. W. Ewing, lieutenant 1st infantry	29.23	Reported to the First Comptroller of the Treasury, for suit, 15th August, 1820.
R. M. Forsyth, lieutenant of artillery	550.00	Ditto ditto 3d June, 1819.
Edward S. Gantt, lieutenant	313.42	Ditto ditto 1st July, 1818.
William Lavall, captain 1st infantry	1,411.00	Called upon, repeatedly, without effect.
R. H. Goodwynn, lieutenant 7th infantry	200.00	Resigned, without settling his accounts. Place of residence unknown.
Nathaniel H. Hall, captain	120.00	Reported to the First Comptroller of the Treasury, for suit, 10th November, 1819.
George W. Murray	11,279.12	Ditto 15th July, 1820. For lead, loaned him in 1815.

TREASURY DEPARTMENT,

Second Auditor's Office, 1st November, 1820.

WM. LEE

No. 2

STATEMENT of Accounts, in the Office of the Third Auditor of the Treasury, which have remained unsettled, or on which balances appear to have been due, more than three years, prior to the 30th September, 1820: furnished in pursuance of the directions contained in the second section of the act of Congress, passed the 3d March, 1809, entitled "An act further to amend the several acts for the establishment and regulation of the Treasury War, and Navy, Departments."

Names and Rank	Amount Dolls.Cts.	Remarks
Anderson, William, lieutenant 1st regiment	313.18	Balance on settlement, 11th Feb. 1820. Claims credit for recruits enlisted, for which the vouchers are wanting.
Andrews, Robert, assistant deputy quartermaster	425.32	Balance on settlement, 21st Nov. 1815, $267.32, and a subsequent advance of $158.
Akerly, Samuel, hospital surgeon	300.00	Advanced him on account of the hospital department, as a fund to pay for hospital stewards, ward masters, and nurses at New York.
Amberson, Silas, captain 22nd	100.00	Advanced him on account of the contingent expenses in recruiting.
Allen, John, lieutenant colonel Kentucky militia	100.00	Advanced him by James Taylor, on account of militia.
Adams, Benjamin, captain	1,840.45	Balance on settlement, 31st Oct. 1816. The balance, according to his statement, is $$687 6. The difference consists in charges not vouched.
Abrahams, Abraham D. military agent	515.66	Balance on settlement 30th March, 1818. Reported for suit.
Armistead, A. B. captain, deceased	1,285.06	Balance on settlement, 17th May, 1811, $58.87 He has received subsequently advances on account of bounties, &c. contingencies and camp equipage, &c. making a balance of $1285 6.
Aitkin, Jonathan W. paymaster 16th	17,907.00	Balance on settlement, 11th October, 1820. Reported for suit.
Anderson, James M. captain 8th	310.00	Balance on settlement, 6th October, 1820. Reported for suit.
Alexander, John B. captain volunteers	800.00	Advanced on account of service of volunteers.
Adams, Nathaniel F. paymaster 4th	24,596.73	Vouchers rendered to the amount of $15,150.35; but no account current, or abstract. He has been required to furnish them prior to settlement.
Allen, Hanibal M. captain	604.00	Advanced on account of bounties, &c.
Allen, William	2,000.00	Advanced him on account of the purchase of real estate for the United States, in the vicinity of Pittsfield, Mass. which will be covered by the conveyances to be made.
Atkin, Thomas, hospital surgeon	400.00	Advanced him on account of contingencies and hospital department.
Austin, Henry B. ensign	34.50	Advanced him on account of transportation of baggage.

Names and Rank	Amount Dolls.Cts.	Remarks
Allen, Nathaniel, deputy paymaster	6,008.21	Apparent balance per account audited, not decided upon by the 2nd Comptroller. The money has been disbursed in payments, which, in the opinion of the Auditor, requires legislative sanction. According to his own statement his account is balanced by refunding in July, 1818, the sum of $4,259.57, the balance in his hands; at which time his accounts were rendered to the paymaster general for settlement.
Armistead, Lewis G. A. captain riflemen	19.63	Balance on settlement, 2d January, 1817.
Allstan, Joseph W. ensign 11th	100.00	Advanced him on account of bounties.
Ayres, Marshall, lieutenant 43d	70.00	Advanced him on account of bounties and contingencies.
Allen, B. C. lieutenant 9th	879.12	Balance on settlement, 16th May, 1820. Has additional claims for bounties to soldiers, the vouchers for which are wanting.
Aiken, James G. ensign 9th	425.56	Balance on settlement, 27th January, 1820. Charges made by him for for bounties without vouchers and money stolen, amounting to nearly the balance.
Albright, Peter, ensign 1st riflemen	12.07	Balance on settlement, 3d June, 1815.
Anspack, P. cornet dragoons	166.00	Advanced on account of bounties, &c.
Allen Watters, assist and D. paymaster	15,874.91	Balance on settlement, 13th March, 1820. Other accounts may probably be to render, the officer being dead none have been received beyond those credited, and his account has been reported for suit.
Andrews, Philo. Assist. Deputy quartermaster general	603.16	Balance on settlement, 9th April, 1816.
Aull, William, lieutenant 4th rifle reg.	231.26	Balance on settlement, 14th September, 1816.
Audrain, James H. captain rangers	26,310.25	Advanced for the payment of his company of rangers, in the service of the United States, during the late war. He claims to have disbursed all the money, but the vouchers produced are in part unsatisfactory; has been required to perfect them.
Armstrong, H. B. major riflemen	349.41	Balance on settlement, 4th April, 1817.
Adams, Joseph C. captain 34th	476.60	Balance on settlement, 30th April, 1817. Suspensions to the amount of $113. for want of vouchers.
Alexander, William, captain	345.72	Balance on settlement, 4th June, 1818. Of this sum $395.92, is for suspensions, the vouchers being imperfect.
Armstrong, John, late rifle reg.	1.84	Balance on settlement, 16th May 1817.
Allison, Uriah, captain 2d riflement	354.65	Balance on settlement, 8th June 1819. Suspensions equal to the balance, which require additional vouchers.

STATEMENT--Continued

Names and Rank	Amount Dolls.Cts.	Remarks
Atchison, George, lieutenant 19th	1, 868.00	Balance on settlement, 4th September, 1817. Reported for suit.
Adams, Parmenio, New York Militia	47,994.19	Accounts rendered. By his statement, he claims a balance of $225.88; but as far as the examination has progressed this is not established. He will probably be indebted for charges made and now allowed, and other items, amounting $704.50.
Addison, Williams H. ensign 38th	426.63	Advanced on account of bounties and contingencies.
Aldridge, Isaac, captain 38th	3,122.42	Balance on settlement, 16th June, 1818. Suspensions to the amount of $212.12. Has additional accounts to render. Reported for suit.
Arrison, John, captain, 23d	371.75	Balance of settlement, 1st June, 1818.
Amelung, Frederick, A. captain 1st	576.00	Balance of his recruiting account. Claims credit for the whole amount, having accounted for it to the commanding officer of his regiment, by paying over the balance to him, of which he to have forwarded evidence, but it cannot be found.
Andrews, Phineas, lieutenant 25th infantry	254.44	Balance on settlement, 19th August, 1818. Suspensions to the amount to the amount of $56, for want of proper vouchers.
Anderson, William P. colonel	4,487.30	Account rendered, but not finally acted on; requires expalanation; and attend in person to the settlement.
Archer, John, lieutenant and paymaster 20th regiment	2,032.74	Balance on settlement, 10th November 1817, $1932.74 and $100 subsequently brought to his, making his balance.
Aspinwall, Thomas, lieutenant colonel	74.87	Advanced him on account of contingencies.
Adams, Daniel, paymaster volunteers	2,312.19	Balance on settlement, 10th July, 1820. Suspensions of charges made by him $1456.85, requiring additional vouchers.
Albright, Jacob W. lieut. And assist. dep. quartermaster	232,988.37	Accounts and vouchers rendered, and in the course of settlement. from his own statement no balance appears due.

STATEMENT--Continued

Names and Rank	Amount Dolls.Cts.	Remarks
Allen, Joseph, paymaster detachment Kentucky militia	99.21	Balance on settlement, 12th March, 1818
Allen, William O. captain, 35th infantry	172.91	Do. Do. 14th July, 1818
Ayer, Lewis M. lieutenant 24th infantry	58.19	Do. Do. 25th May, 1818. Has claims for items suspended for want of proper vouchers amounting to $24.
Adams, Littleton, paymaster 3d Ohio Militia	763.59	Do. Do. 15th September, 1819.
Ashton, Abraham C. paymaster New York Militia	158.51	Do. Do. 2d December, 1819. In suit.
Allen, George C. lieutenant 7th	86.95	Do. Do. 29th May, 1818. Suspensions to amount of this balance for want of proper vouchers.
Atherton, Joseph H. lieutenant 31st	455.00	Advanced him on account of bounties, &c.
Albro, Samuel E. ensign 31st	530.00	Advanced on account of bounties and contingencies.
Appling, Daniel, captain 4th riflemen	796.95	Advanced on account of bounties and contingencies.
Armstrong, John, brigadier general	1,759.43	This charge is for expenses for himself and suite on a journey to the lines, in the fall of 1813, which he states to have been expended; will render accounts and vouches therefore, as promised on an application to account for the money.
Adair, William I. captain 17th	1,890.00	Advanced for bounties and premiums, and contingencies.
Alexander, Marshall T.	34.82	Balance on settlement, 13 August, 118. Claims a balance which cannot be allowed for want of vouchers.
Aldrick, Timothy, lieutenant 11th	949.91	Do. Do. 14th August, 1818. Claims credits to the amount of $215, not admissible for want of vouchers.
Atwood, Jon, lieutenant 31st	157.85	Do. Do. 22nd Aug, 1818. Has claims to this amount requiring additional vouchers.
Austin, Thomas C. paymaster South Carolina militia	19,000.00	Accounts rendered and under examination. His own balance has been refunded.
Armistead, William A. paymaster Virginia militia	1,205.78	Balance on settlement, 8th August, 1820. Suspensions to the amount of $737.16, additional evidence wanting.
Anderson, Robert, lieutenant 26th	94.80	Do. Do. 25th August 1819, $44.80; he is since charged with $50 in addition thereto.
Annin, Samuel, paymaster Harper's Ferry	15,503.83	Do. Do. 12th October, 1820. Makes additional claims which cannot be admitted. Reported for suit.
Allen, Ethan A. late assis. dep. quartermaster general	433.17	Balance on settlement, 15th January, 1819. Has rendered additional vouchers amounting to $68, and claims credit for others lost In the Ohio river amounting to $140.
Avery, John C. lieutenant 26th	510.00	Advanced on account of bounties and contingencies.

STATEMENT--Continued

Names and Rank	Amount Dolls.Cts.	Remarks
Anderson, Acquilla B. paymaster 41st Maryland militia	8,575.53	Balance on settlement, 26th Feb. 1819. Has additional accounts to to render. Reported for suit 21st October, 1820.
Awl, James, ensign 16th	263.20	Do. Do. 23d July 1819.
Armistead, George colonel	1,000.00	Advanced by paymaster general on account of bounties, &c.
Arrel, Richard, lieutenant 14th	110.00	Advanced on account of bounties and pay of the army.
Armstrong, John, lieutenant 22d	20.00	Advanced on account of bounties, &c.
Brent, Robert, paymaster general	40,911.18	Balance on settlement, 2d June, 1820. Reported for suit.
Boyd, Joseph C. deputy paymaster	347,039.99	Accounts and vouchers rendered, not yet examined. The balance which he admits himself, has been refunded.
Blair, Thomas, ensign 11th	11.68	Balance on settlement, 7th February, 1815.
Bell, Richard H. lieutenant 5th	242.00	Advanced on account of pay of the army and contingencies.
Brasfield, Wiley R. paymaster Kentucky militia	136.38	Balance on settlement, 30th March, 1820. Suspensions to the amount of $110.68 requiring additional vouchers.

STATEMENT--Continued

Names and Rank	Amount Dolls.Cts.	Remarks
Bruce, Bailey, lieutenant 12th	916.75	Balance on settlement, 6th September, 1816. Suspensions to the amount of $547.77 for want of additional vouchers.
Byers, James, contractor 6th November, 1811	10.00	On account of subsistence, it being a balance overpaid him on settlement, 24th August, 1815.
Bridges, George R. lieutenant 10th	928.84	Balance on settlement, 19th October, 1816. Suspensions $635.12, requiring additional vouchers, though the money has been paid.
Bacon, Benedict, quartermaster Kentucky militia	75.00	Advanced on account of the militia.
Bailey, William, lieutenant	56.48	Advanced on account of contingencies.
Burbeck, Henry, colonel	60.96	Payment made by the quartermaster for furniture for his quarters, charged to his personal account.
Beeman, Joseph, Jun. captain	353.00	Advanced on account of bounties, &c.
Brown, Return B. captain 24th	1,390.00	Accounts rendered, but no vouchers, which he has been called upon for. His charges would apparently leave a balance of $500 unaccounted for.
Bean, Richard, lieutenant	44.70	Balance on settlement, 11th June, 1814.
Blanchard, William, lieutenant 19th	600.00	Advanced on account of pay of the army, bounties, and contingencies.
Brady, Josiah, lieutenant 26th	455.00	Advanced on account of bounties and contingencies.
Bell, John C. ensign, 34th	8.00	Advanced on account of contingencies.
Blake, Oliver, ensign 34th	324.73	Accounts rendered without vouchers, for 100 dollars, making the apparent balance due $224.73.
Buff, Thomas, contract of making musket balls	500.00	Advanced him on account of ordnance, for making balls. Insolvent.
Butler, John. Captain 2d dragoons	4800.00	Advanced on account of pay, bounties, and quartermaster department. Reported for suit.
Binns, John A. lieutenant 1st dragoons	1900.00	Balance on settlement, 12th August, 1820. Promises to render his accounts.
Butts, David C. captain 31st	34.00	do. do. 12th December, 1816.
Burr, Levi S. lieutenant 23d	3807.26	do. do. 21st October, 1820. 185 dollars suspended for want of proper vouchers. Reported for suit.
Bartlett, Josiah, lieutenant 21st	545.60	do. do. 28th October, 1816. He claims additional credit to nearly this amount, part of which was deducted, not admissible, and others suspended, amounting to $160.70, for additional vouchers.
Brooks, Henry, lieutenant	100.00	Advanced on account of bounties, &c.
Blue, Uriah, captain 7th	450.00	Advanced on account of bounties, &c.

STATEMENT--Continued

Names and Rank	Amount Dolls.Cts.	Remarks
Branton, N. lieutenant 7th	50.00	Advanced on account of bounties, &c.
Bixbee, Moses, jun.	100.00	Advanced on account of volunteers.
Botts, George W. paymaster Kentucky militia		Balance on settlement, 15th June, 1820.
Boothe, Sylvester, ensign 2d dragoons	4083.00	do. do. 2d August, 1820. Suspensions $314.61. Reported for suit.
Blaise, Francis, ensign 23d	760.00	Vouchers rendered, and apparently amounting to 222 dollars. No statement; has been called upon for additional vouchers and accounts.
Brodwater, William E. lieutenant 2d artillery	400.00	Accounts rendered in part, amounting to 24 dollars. Has been required to forward his accounts and vouchers.
Boote, William R. captain 2d	1.50	Balance on settlement, 25th March, 1813.
Borden, Samuel, lieut. And quartermaster 4th infantry	975.50	Advanced him on account of camp equipage, &c.
Brooks, Jonathan, captain 6th	863.50	Balance on settlement, 26th September, 1816. Suspensions to the amount of 206 dollars, for want of proper vouchers.

STATEMENT--Continued

Names and Rank	Amount Dolls.Cts.	Remarks
Ballinger, John, captain, 24th	3151.50	Balance on settlement, 26th October, 1816. Reported for suit 23d September, 1819.
Beall, Thomas J. lieutenant artillery	1558.86	Written to on the subject of this balance. No answer.
Bird, Ross, captain 3d	200.00	Advanced him on account of bounties, &c. Dead.
Bell, George M. lieutenant 17th	770.00	Accounts rendered without vouchers for $68.80, and apparent balance due $701.20 dollars.
Branch, Henry, captain 20th	564.58	Balance on settlement, 10th June, 1813.
Britton, P. captain	40.01	do. do. 16th August, 1816.
Brown, Henry lieutenant	50.00	Advanced him on account of contingencies.
Bradley, Peter, captain	2740.00	Accounts rendered without vouchers, for 600 dollars; apparent balance 2140 dollars.
Buck, Londus L. lieutenant 6th infantry	1122.00	Balance on settlement, 3d April, 1820. Suspensions to amount of 66 dollars, requiring additional vouchers.
Bucklin, Rufus, lieutenant 11th	154.19	do. do. 28th June, 1816.
Black, James A. lieutenant 8th	1086.06	do. do. 16th December, 1816.
Bailey, Thomas S.	233.38	do. do. 14th March, 1816.
Beebe, Ebenezer, captain, deceased	1891.04	Advanced on account of clothing and bounties, &c. Has doubtless applied the greater part of the balance, by reports received; but no account or vouchers rendered.
Barneville, Edward, lieutenant 34th	505.52	Balance on settlement, 13th December, 1816. Suspensions to the Amount of $429.31, requiring additional evidence.
Burnard, Julius, lieutenant dragoons,	300.00	Advanced on account of bounties and contingencies.
Bryan, Peter, lieutenant 28th	668.85	Balance on settlement, 9th November, 1816. Has suspensions to amount of 612 dollars, for want of additional vouchers.
Barker, James N. captain 2d artillery	5274.81	do. do. 21st September, 1820. Promises to render other accounts.
Byrd, Francis O. lieutenant 2d artillery	450.00	Accounts rendered without vouchers off $176.50, and apparent balance due, $273.50.
Bender, Henry, lieutenant 21st	50.00	Advanced on account of bounties, &c.
Blasdell, N. lieutenant	36.05	Balance on settlement, 26th February, 1815.
Burghardt, Adolphus, ensign 9th	350.00	Accounts rendered for $81.67, without vouchers; apparent balance due $268.33.
Barbour, Philip, lieutenant colonel militia	3909.00	Advanced him on account of the pay of his regiment of militia. Has doubtless applied the greater part, if not the whole; but has rendered no evidence thereof. Dead.

STATEMENT--Continued

Names and Rank	Amount Dolls.Cts.	Remarks
Bayley, Robert P. United States factor	565.00	Advanced on account of contingencies.
Brown, John, forage master militia	60.00	Advanced on account of quartermaster department.
Brown, Jeremiah, ensign	20.00	Advanced on account of contingencies.
Bache, Richard, captain volunteer artillery	100.00	Advanced on account of quartermaster department.
Barnett, Joseph, Kentucky militia	820.87	Balance on settlement, 27th October, 1820. Suspensions to nearly this amount for want of vouchers.
Barnett, Joseph, lieutenant 20th	434.00	Advanced on account of bounties and contingencies.
Brown, Andrew	40.00	Advanced on account of militia.
Berryman, Walter, lieutenant 2d artillery	64.05	Balance on settlement, 22d June, 1816, $4.05; and a subsequent advance of $60, on account of contingencies.
Bayley, James, lieutenant 6th	358.00	Advanced on account of bounties, pay, contingencies, and quartermaster department.

STATEMENT--Continued

Names and Rank	Amount Dolls.Cts.	Remarks
Brooks, Jonas G. ensign	28.00	Balance on settlement, 22d October, 1816. Has suspensions equal to this balance, requiring additional vouchers.
Butterfield, Jonathan, lieutenant	16.00	Balance on settlement, 28th October, 1816. Suspensions amounting to $16 for want of the proper vouchers.
Baxter, Stephen, New York volunteers	58,676.60	Act passed for his relief, called upon for the necessary statements; Not furnished, no balance will be due in this case.
Berry, Joseph, ensign	120.00	Balance on settlement 16th December, 1816.
Butler, W. captain 3d infantry	1,162.00	Advanced him on account of bounties, &c.
Bell, Henry, lieutenant 28th	425.00	Accounts rendered for $36.75 without vouchers; apparent balance due $388.25.
Booker, Daniel, lieutenant 20th	1,162.00	Advanced him on account of bounties, &c.
Baldwin, Ira, pilot	50.00	Advanced him on account of quartermaster department.
Bender, Joseph, lieutenant 32d	133.33	Advanced on account of bounties and contingencies.
Buck, Daniel, A. A. captain 31st	89.76	Balance on settlement 1st December, 1816. Suspensions amounting to $47.22 for want of proper vouchers.
Baker, Asa, lieutenant 31st	158.71	Do. do. 27th August, 1816. Suspensions to the amount of $108.75 requiring additional vouchers.
Burnap, Ethan, captain, 31st	226.66	Do. do. 2d December, 1816.
Blount, William A. lieutenant 18th	233.34	Accounts rendered and claims a balance.
Blackstone, Thomas, ensign 7th	400.00	Advanced on account of pay, bounties, and contingencies.
Byers, John, contractor	5,034.19	Balance on settlement 29th October, 1816. Suspensions to amount of $590.51 requiring additional vouchers. Reported for suit.
Baylor, Cyrus A. lieutenant 17th	1,150.00	Accounts rendered amounting to $538.76 not supported by vouchers; Apparent balance due $611.23.
Berry, Samuel S. lieutenant 17th	178.13	Balance on settlement 26th September, 1816. Suspensions amounting to $52.50 requiring further vouchers.
Berringer, Philip, lieutenant	40.00	Advanced on account of militia.
Barker, Peleg, captain sea fencibles	134.40	Balance on settlement 3d February, 1820. Suspensions amounting to $52.50 requiring further vouchers.
Baynton, Edward, lieutenant 3d artillery	500.00	Advanced on account of bounties, &c.
Buck, Samuel, Fredericksburg, Virginia	226.27	Advanced on account of quartermaster department.
Balch, Samuel G. lieutenant 24th	300.00	Advanced on account of pay, bounties, and contingencies.
Bouten, Narcissus, lieutenant 7th	200.00	Advanced on account of bounties, &c.

STATEMENT--Continued

Names and Rank	Amount Dolls.Cts.	Remarks
Badger, Edward, lieutenant 9th	1,177.00	Balance on settlement 5th April 1820. Suspensions for want of proper vouchers amounting to $186; has since rendered accounts and vouchers for $811.83 and has others to render.
Browning, William, ensign 9th	78.69	Balance on settlement 19th, February, 1820.
Boothe, E. E.	300.00	Advanced on account of quartermaster department.
Boland, Noah	120.00	Advanced on account of quartermaster department.
Bourke, Walter, lieutenant 3d infantry	800.00	Advanced on account of bounties, &c.
Burnett, Joseph D.	100.00	Balance on settlement 26th September, 1815.
Ball, James V. lieutenant colonel	67.50	Advanced on account of quartermaster department.
Belding, G. H. lieutenant 5th	40.00	Advanced on account of contingencies.
Boyd, John P. brigadier general	120.29	Advanced on account of quartermaster department.
Barnett, William R. captain	29.37	Balance on settlement 27th January, 1816.

STATEMENT--Continued

Names and Rank	Amount Dolls.Cts.	Remarks
Beckett, John, lieutenant	25.00	Advanced on account of quartermaster department.
Benedict, Ebenezer, lieutenant 27th	594.00	Advanced on account of bounties and contingencies.
Boynton, B. A. lieutenant 29th	40.40	Advanced on account of quartermaster department.
Brownson, Gideon, lieutenant 30th	8.00	Advanced on account of bounties, &c.
Bronaugh, James C. surgeon	70.00	Advanced on account of quartermaster department.
Beall, William D. colonel 36th	816.95	Balance on settlement 13th April, 1816
Blackledge, Thomas W. lieutenant 3d rifle	4,200.00	Advanced on account of bounties, contingencies, and Quartermaster department.
Burr, Samuel, ensign, 29th	500.00	Advanced on account of bounties, &c.
Bennett, Abijah, lieutenant 23d	129.56	Balance on settlement 22d May, 1816.
Buckley, Thomas W. lieutenant 11th	278.38	Do. do. 4th Nov. 1816. Suspensions amounting to $83.62 for which vouchers are wanting.
Baylor, William, lieutenant 17th	490.00	Accounts rendered and claims a balance.
Brown, Walter B. ensign 11th	109.82	Balance on settlement 29th June, 1816. Suspensions to a greater amount than the balance, requiring vouchers.
Blair, William P. ensign 28th	100.00	Advanced on account of bounties, &c.
Burton, George, lieutenant 18th	46.13	Balance on settlement 3d October, 1817, $12 and do. 26th March, 1817 $34.13--$12 suspended for want of vouchers.
Blanchard, Reuben K. lieutenant 40th	278.80	Balance on settlement 26 March, 1817, $74.80, suspensions amounting to $51.81 for want of vouchers; he has since been charged with $204, making the balance.
Berry, Peter, lieutenant colonel	100.00	Advanced on account of contingencies.
Bill, Alexander F. F. lieutenant	2,828.24	Balance on settlement 14th April 1820. He states that he has lost his vouchers for which he means to apply to Congress. Reported for suit 28th September, 1820.
Baskerville, E. B. ensign	346.00	Advanced on account of pay, bounties, and contingencies.
Bartlett, David	1,858.00	Advanced on account of bounties and contingencies.
Beall, Elias, captain 43d infantry	66.35	Balance on settlement, 28th March, 1817. Suspensions amounting to $64, requiring additional proof.
Bartlett, John C. late quartermaster general	22,754.82	Balance on settlement, 30th September 1819. Reported for suit, 5th October, 1819.
Bryson, James W. assis.dep. quartermaster general	22,155.33	He stands charged on the books, with the sum $22,128.75, and in to which $26.58 on settlement 26th April, 1820, making the balance; suspensions for further vouchers, $16. Reported for suit, 27th September, 1819.

STATEMENT--Continued

Names and Rank	Amount Dolls.Cts.	Remarks
Brown, Daniel, colonel 23d	9,585.56	Balance on settlement, 3d August, 1820, Reported for suit.
Brown, Samuel, major	2,789.76	Do. do. 2d August, 1820. Vouchers suspended for additional proof, amounting to nearly this balance.
Bleeker, John, deputy quartermaster general	15,798.00	Balance on settlement, 10th July 1818, $10,298.59. He has since received $5,500. Reported for suit. Additional accounts rendered; under examination.
Butler, Anthony, colonel	1,340.19	Balance on settlement, 28th May, 1817, $1,310.19, other moneys have subsequently been brought to his debt, making the balance. Has a claim for arrears of pay, &c. not rendered to this office.
Brady, Samuel	12.00	Advanced on account of bounties &c.

STATEMENT--Continued

Names and Rank	Amount Dolls.Cts.	Remarks
Babcock, H. C. lieutenant	1,350.00	Balance on settlement, 19th September, 1820. Reported for suit, 28th September, 1820.
Butler, Thomas L. captain 28th	168.56	Do. do. 19th May 1817. Suspensions to amount of $152. for want of proper vouchers.
Berry, Thomas lieutenant 2d riflemen	562.94	Do. do. 31 July, 1818. Suspensions to amount of $360. not properly vouched.
Bayley, John, lieutenant colonel	42.00	Advanced on account of quartermaster department.
Billings, E. B. lieutenant 44th	575.77	Balance on settlement, 23d May, 1817. Suspensions to amount of $116 requiring further proof.
Bumford, Thomas, lieutenant 7th	33.31	Do. do. 24th May, 1817. Suspensions to amount of $28.75, for which vouchers are wanting
Bryan, Willis N. ensign 28th	41.77	Do. do. 18th May, 1820.
Brown, Daniel G. ensign 28th	938.00	Balance on settlement, 18th November, 1818. $228 suspended for want of additional vouchers.
Britton, James, captain 14th	399.30	Do. do. 10th June, 1817. Suspensions, for want of proper vouchers, amount to more than this balance.
Beasley, Reuben G. agent for pensions	3,428.86	Balance on settlement, 6th August, 1918. Reported for suit.
Burnes, Hector, ensign 16th	163.65	Do. do. 8th September, 1818. Suspensions to a greater amount than this balance, for want of the necessary vouchers.
Biddle, John, captain 42d	85.00	Advanced on account of bounties and contingencies.
Branch, Benjamin, captain artillery	100.00	Advanced on account of bounties, &c.
Bird, William C. lieutenant 5th	349.83	Balance on settlement, 31st August, 1817. $208.83, suspensions, for want of vouchers, exceed the balance on this settlement. Has since had an advance on account of pay of the of the army, for $141, not embraced in the above settlement.
Boyle, James H. captain artillery	100.00	Advanced on account of bounties, &c.
Blake, Henry J. lieutenant 11th infantry	1,140.00	Advanced on account of pay, bounties, contingencies, and quartermaster department.
Bucklin, Joseph, captain 9th	1,217.00	Balance on settlement, 12th November, 1819. Reported for suit, 24th November, 1819.
Barbour, Isaac B. captain, 9th	213.98	Do. do. 10th September, 1817. Suspensions amounting to $101.80, for want of additional vouchers.

STATEMENT--Continued

Names and Rank	Amount Dolls.Cts.	Remarks
Booker, Richard, captain volunteers	60.00	Advanced on account of contingencies.
Biddle, Thomas captain	451.57	Balance on settlement, 24th February, 1819.
Butterfield, Shubal, lieutenant 5th	1,169.32	Balance on settlement, 11th October, 1817. Suspensions amounting to $120, requiring additional vouchers. Reported for suit 3d October, 1820.
Brook, George M. major 23d	6,953.20	Advanced on account of bounties, contingencies, pay, quartermaster department, and camp equipements, &c. He states that he has lost his accounts and vouchers. Legislative interference necessary.
Belmear, Francis, act. paymaster, Maryland militia	11.48	Balance on settlement, 2d October, 1817.
Bryant, Daniel C. captain, 31st	334.26	Do. do. 10th November 1817. Suspensions to amount of $269.24 for want of additional vouchers.
Baker, Marshall, lieutenant 45th	4.00	Do. do. 27 November, 1817.
Banister, Seth, captain, 9th	971.00	Do. do. 11th August, 1817. $100 suspended for want of proper vouchers. Reported for suit 27th September, 1820.
Bean, Stephen, captain, 33d	297.16	Balance on settlement, 10th December, 1817. Suspensions amounting to $156.50, requiring additional vouchers.

STATEMENT--Continued

Names and Rank	Amount Dolls.Cts.	Remarks
Beall, Jonathan, assistant deputy paymaster,	5,875.43	Balance on settlement, 16th December, 1819. Suspensions amounting to $130.40, requiring additional vouchers.
Barlow, Jesse	200.00	Advanced on account of contingencies.
Brent, George, ensign 5th	600.00	Advanced on account of bounties and contingencies.
Bucker, Bailey, ensign	169.00	Balance on settlement, 28th March, 1820. Suspensions amounting to $10 for want of vouchers.
Bryan, George, lieutenant 16th	2,500.00	Accounts rendered without vouchers for $1,172.62, making apparent balance due $1,130.78.
Burnside, J. M. lieutenant 16th	1,400.00	Accounts rendered for $269.22 without vouchers, making apparent balance due $1,130.78.
Baldwin, Larkin L. ensign 43d	23.05	Balance on settlement, 9th March, 1818. Amount of suspensions is greater than the balance requiring vouchers.
Blount, Willie, governor	10,015.78	Do. do. 10th April, 1818.
Bodley, Thomas, quartermaster gen. Kentucky militia	28,135.42	Do. do. 21st June, 1820. Reported for suit.
Boyd, Alexander H. late paymaster 5th Md. Militia	131.27	Do. do. 13th April, 1819. Suspensions amounting to $49.54 requiring additional vouchers.
Butler, Paul D. Ohio militia	500.00	Advanced on account of the pay of the Ohio militia. No account rendered.
Belton, Francis S. paymaster 1st light dragoons	42,035.59	Account rendered, and apparent balance $442.66, as paymaster and additional vouchers for recruiting purposes amounting to $110.51.
Brearly, Benjamin, lieutenant	1,372.00	Accounts rendered, amounting to $585.67, without vouchers, and apparent balance due $786.33.
Bartlett, John P. lieutenant 3d artillery	1,121.92	Balance on settlement 29th October, 1818; suspensions amounting to $740.77, for want of proper vouchers.
Bostick, John G lieutenant 8th	374.99	Ditto. 21st October, 1818.
Belknap, Augustus, paymaster N. Y. militia	425.27	Reported for suit 5th June, 1818.
Brown, Simon, lieutenant 31st	169.93	Balance on settlement 27th August, 1819; suspensions to amount of $57, requiring additional vouchers.
Brown, Amos. W. lieutenant 31st	509.25	Balance on settlement 21st July, 1820. suspensions to amount of $70, requiring vouchers. Has further claims.
Briggs, Isaac, ensign 31st	54.39	Balance on settlement 1st May, 1819.
Bohonnon, Ebenezer W. ensign 31st	400.00	Advanced on account of bounties, &c.
Baird, William captain 19th	13.00	Balance on settlement 17th May, 1820.
Brearly, David, colonel 15th	1,188.36	Balance on settlement 17th July, 1820.

STATEMENT--Continued

Names and Rank	Amount Dolls.Cts.	Remarks
Barton, Joseph L captain 15th	1,650.00	Accounts rendered for $192.48, without vouchers, making apparent balance due $1,457.52.
Buckner, Wm. H. doctor	26.60	Advanced on account of quartermaster department.
Babcock, L. S. captain	855.50	Balance on settlement 19th September, 1820. Reported for suit.
Brown, Gabriel H. wagon master	420.00	Advanced on account of quartermaster department
Brown, William	400.00	Advanced on account of quartermaster department.
Burr, Timothy, captain &c.	39,799.60	Accounts rendered, which are informal, and require additional vouchers, amounting in his statement to $32,099.65, leaving an apparent balance due $7,699.95. He claims $7,250 for money lost.
Bourke, Thomas, quartermaster general, Georgia	25,814.34	Balance on settlement, October, 1820; suspensions made on his account amounting in his statement to $22,710.90,which require additional vouchers.
Bruce, Amasa J. lieutenant 12th	1,787.26	Balance on settlement 11th November, 1819; suspensions amounting to $54; not supported by vouchers. Reported for suit 24th November, 1819.
Boyden, Alvan, lieutenant 45th	54.00	Balance on settlement 1st September, 1818.

STATEMENT--Continued

Names and Rank	Amount Dolls.Cts.	Remarks
Burton, John H. lieutenant 30th	508.08	Balance on settlement, 2d September, 1818; suspensions amounting to $240.19, for want of additional vouchers. Reported for suit.
Brimhall, Elisha, lieutenant 9th	92.00	Balance on settlement, 11th September, 1818.
Blackley, Moses, captain 13th	244.00	Balance on settlement, 14th September, 1818, suspensions to amount of $164, requiring proper vouchers. Reported for suit 24th December, 1819.
Boerstler, George W. paymaster 1st Maryland militia	2,089.82	Balance on settlement, 26th September, 1818; suspensions amounting to $1,790.72, requiring additional vouchers.
Butler, Thomas,	550.00	Advanced on account of quartermaster dep't, and for the purpose of procuring supplies for Virginia militia.
Benjamin, Caleb, captain, &c.	1,998.54	Balance on settlement, 1st October, 1818. Reported for suit 23d September, 1819.
Bacon, Josiah, lieutenant 4th infantry	2,423.44	Accounts rendered for $76.75, without vouchers; leaving the apparent balance due $2,246.69.
Bedel, Moody, lieutenant colonel	12,700.21	Balance on settlement, 21st September, 1819.
Battle, Hollyman, lieutenant 43d	560.63	Balance on settlement, 20th November, 1818; suspensions amounting to $60 for want of vouchers. Reported for suit 20th October, 1819.
Bugbee, Luther, lieutenant 31st	11.40	Balance on settlement, 29th December, 1818; suspensions amounting to $10, vouchers wanting.
Bradshaw, James, paymaster 1st Ky. Vol. dragoons	32.75	Balance on settlement, 3d February, 1819.
Boardman, E. captain 26th	366.50	Advanced on account of contingencies.
Brett, Robert, lieutenant	250.00	Advanced on account of bounties, &c.
Burrill, William, lieutenant, 13th	2,782. 7	Balance on settlement, 16th December, 1818; the sum of $40 suspended for further proof.
Bryson, John H captain 1st infantry	912.45	Do. 24th April, 1819; suspensions amounting to $27.47, requiring additional vouchers.
Bartlett, Sandford, ensign	380.00	Advanced on account of bounties, &c.
Butts, Samuel	3,800.00	Advanced on account of quartermaster department.
Bird, John, lieutenant 10th	720.40	Balance on settlement, 5th May, 1819; suspensions amounting to $715.26, for want of proper vouchers. Reported for suit.
Bryant, Samuel H. lieutenant	190.00	Advanced on account of contingencies.
Bryant, Joseph, captain 10th	519.61	Balance on settlement, 5th May, 1819.

STATEMENT--Continued

Names and Rank	Amount Dolls.Cts.	Remarks
Blair, James, lieutenant 19th	258.00	Balance on settlement, 17th May, 1819; suspensions to amount of $120, requiring further proof.
Brown, James, lieutenant 7th	96.00	Do 24th June, 1819; amount of suspensions equal to this balance, for want of vouchers.
Bogardus, Robert, colonel 41st	984.00	Do 28th October, 1819; has promised to refund the balance.
Billings, William, captain	789.17	Do 12th July, 1819, and reported for suit 29th October, 1819.
Bingham, William, lieutenant 31st	128.17	Do 18th September, 1819; amount of suspensions $104.82, requiring further vouchers.
Bangs, Thomas, ensign 9th	274.00	Advanced on account of bounties and contingencies.
Bull, John G. paymaster Pennsylvania militia	19,536.48	Accounts and vouchers rendered and informal.
Burne, Andrew, to pay Virginia militia	1,595.84	Advanced by paymaster general on account of pay, subsistence, and forage.
Bean, N. G. lieutenant 21st	36.79	Balance on settlement 9th August, 1819. Has an account for arrearages to settle with the paymaster general, equal to this balance.

STATEMENT--Continued

Names and Rank	Amount Dolls.Cts.	Remarks
Bayley, John, paymaster 57th Virginia militia	17.71	Balance on settlement 23d September, 1820.
Blanton, Richard, paymaster 5th Kentucky militia	8,210.71	Accounts rendered, but irregular and defective. Written to on the subject of his accounts.
Bennett, Richard, lieutenant 4th infantry	.57	Advanced him on account of bounties, contracts, and quartermaster department, $430.23, and he has since refunded to the paymaster general $429.66; leaving a balance of 57 cents against him.
Boswell, Thomas E. lieutenant 28th	700.00	Advanced on account of bounties, &c.
Brooks, Frederick, captain sea fencibles	63.07	Balance on settlement, 17th September, 1819.
Beard, William C. captain	30.00	Advanced on account of pay of the army.
Bradford, Lemuel, captain, 21st	1,080.01	Advanced on account of bounties, pay, and quartermaster department.
Benton, Thomas H. lieutenant colonel 39th	384.05	Balance on settlement, 11th May, 1820. Reported for suit, 20th October, 1819.
Bacon, Timothy, lieutenant 34th	191.24	Advanced on account of bounties, &c.
Berrian, Samuel, captain 41st	513.74	Balance on settlement, 31st August, 1820, Reported for suit.
Bush, John S. lieutenant artillery	800.44	Do. do. 29th October, 1819. Reported for suit, 5th November, 1819.
Bigelow, Aaron, ensign 21st	675.24	Do. do. 29th October, 1819. Reported for suit, 10th November, 1819.
Barbour, Gabriel, lieutenant dragoons	1,770.00	Do. do. do. Reported for suit, 5th November, 1819
Butler, William, captain, 3d artillery	1,178.00	Do. do. do. do. do.
Burnett, John, lieutenant and quartermaster 3d infantry	1,666.25	Do. do. do. do. do.
Bailey, Thomas, lieutenant 34th	1,261.37	Do. do. do. do. do.
Burgess, John M. lieutenant 36th	700.00	Do. do. do. do. 10th November, 1819.
Baldwin, Thomas P. paymaster New York militia	12,282.50	Do. do. do. Suspensions amounting to $393.81, for want of additional vouchers. Reported for suit.
Bostwick, Benjamin R. late barrack master	5,649.60	Balance on settlement, 9th November, 1819.
Butler, William O. captain 44th	20.00	Advanced on account of quartermaster department.

STATEMENT--Continued

Names and Rank	Amount Dolls.Cts.	Remarks
Beall, Robert, late 14th	2,553.00	Balance on settlement, 9th December, 1819. Suspensions requiring additional vouchers amount to $993.
Brooks, A. S. captain 3d artillery	134.45	Do.　do.　　　17th January 1820.
Blauvelt, Daniel A. paymaster New York militia	63.67	Do.　do.　　　3d February, 1820. Suspensions amounting to $34.38, for want of vouchers.
Carberry, Henry, colonel 36th	2,961.72	Balance on settlement, 7th October, 1820. Amount of suspensions $623. 4.
Crawford, Reuben, lieutenant 20th	472.53	Balance on settlement, 8th March, 1817. Suspensions amounting to $24.81. May have a claim for pay, &c.
Calhoun, James, junr. Balt. Deceased	1,416.00	Advanced on account of quartermaster department, and ordnance, $1,396 of which was advanced on a bill of exchange in favor of James Beatty, navy agent, and drawn by Jno. Gordon, on account of quartering troops in his rope walks, in the fall of 1814.
Camp, John G. lieutenant 12th infantry	300.00	Advanced him on account of contingencies.
Clinton, Owen, captain 10th	878.98	Balance on settlement, 7th of February, 1820. Amount of suspensions $12.
Carr, William W. lieutenant 13th	739.11	Balance on settlement, 16th July, 1814, and 21st September, 1816, $704.11, and an advance of $35, on account of quartermaster department, States that he will be on in March, to attend to his account.
Cogswell, William, forage master	2,450.00	Advanced on account of quartermaster department.

Names and Rank	Amount Dolls.Cts.	Remarks
Chase, Jonathan, quartermaster Virginia militia	30.00	Advanced on account of medical and hospital department.
Childress, Lemuel, ensign 39th	200.00	Advanced on account of bounties, &c.
Corning, Malachi, lieutenant 11th	468.00	Advanced on account of bounties, &c.
Cassidy, Charles	750.00	Advanced on account of contingencies.
Carney, D. L. ensign 19th	651.94	Balance on settlement, 12th November, 1816. Suspensions equal to this amount.
Cratton, Isaac, lieutenant 10th	25.00	Advanced on account of contingencies.
Canty, Samuel B. lieutenant 18th	2.00	Balance on settlement, 23d September, 1813.
Crooker, Calvin, lieutenant 34th	180.00	Accounts rendered, without vouchers, for $80.83; leaving the apparent balance of $99.17.
Crossman, Daniel, captain 34th	233.08	Accounts rendered, without vouchers, for $119.86; leaving the apparent balance of $113.22.
Clark, Thomas, lieutenant 34th	585.00	Accounts rendered, without vouchers, for $367.63; leaving the apparent balance of $217.37.
Chadwick, Peter, captain 34th	3,103.01	Balance on settlement, 28th September, 1819, $6103. He subsequently refunded to the paymaster general $3000, leaving the stated balance. Suspensions $196.43.
Chalmers, James G. paymaster volunteers	255.58	Vouchers rendered, but no account or abstract. He has received other moneys not yet at his debit; making an apparent balance of $28,828.77.
Carney, John, ensign 10th	24.00	Advanced on account of contingencies
Carroll, William B. lieutenant 36th	448.00	Advanced him on account of bounties, &c.
Craig, Samuel H. ensign 17th	901.04	Accounts rendered for $578.91, of which $58 is vouched; leaving an apparent balance of $322.13.
Clark, William, lieutenant 23d	1,176.02	Balance on settlement, 16th September, 1816. Amount of suspensions greater than the balance.
Churchill, Worthy L. lieutenant colonel militia	120.00	Advanced on account of pay of the army.
Crouch, Henry, captain	80.00	Advanced on account of pay of the army.
Case, Nathaniel, captain New York militia	80.00	Advanced on account of pay of the army.
Clark, Joseph, lieutenant militia	60.00	Advanced on account of pay of the army.
Case, James, lieutenant militia	60.00	Advanced on account of pay of the army.
Church, Jesse, lieutenant New York militia	60.00	Advanced on account of pay of the army.
Campbell, John, ensign 2d infantry	142.29	Balance on settlement, 9th August, 1811.
Coles, Walter, lieutenant 2d dragoons	140.23	Do do 1st July, 1815.
Cooper, John, surgeon's mate	25.50	Advanced on account of contingencies.

STATEMENT--Continued

Names and Rank	Amount Dolls.Cts.	Remarks
Cock, William captain, 6th	151.09	Balance on settlement, 15th August, 1812, on account of camp equipage, $51.09, and an advance of $100 on account of contingencies.
Cross, Joseph, captain artillery	221.52	Advanced on account of bounties, camp equipage, &c.
Cheny, Samuel, lieutenant, deceased	134.40	Advanced on account of camp equipage, &c.
Constant, Joseph, lieutenant colonel	51.00	Advanced him on account of subsistence, drawn as double rations, not allowed.
Cross, Ebenezer, captain 6th	212.60	Advanced on account of subsistence and contingencies.
Campbell, John, lieutenant 1st	40.00	Advanced him on account of contingencies.
Carter, Robert B. contractor	58,519.61	Accounts and vouchers rendered, upon which he claims a balance of $3,198.90.

STATEMENT--Continued

Names and Rank	Amount Dolls.Cts.	Remarks
Corporation of New York	723.86	Advanced on account of contingencies, by Governor Tompkins.
Conrad, Robert R. lieutenant riflemen	4,141.87	Balance on settlement, 27th March, 1820. Has other accounts to render, which, he states, will be shortly furnished.
Copeland, Jesse, captain 10th, deceased	119.61	Balance on settlement, 15th March, 1820
Chisholm, William, captain, 8th	673.71	Do. do. 16th November, 1816; suspensions amounting to $663.12.
Clark, Robert, lieutenant 4th	700.03	Do. do. 5th October, 1816; suspensions amounting to $410.67; states that he has lost his vouchers on board the Chippewa.
Chrystie, James, lieutenant 14th	647.53	Balance on settlement, 26th September, 1816, $571.53, and a subsequent advance of $75; suspensions amounting to $365.25.
Chipman, Samuel, lieutenant	416.23	Balance on settlement, 2d July, 1813, and 13th February, 1817; suspensions, $54.
Crawford, Charles, captain 8th	1,004.48	Do. do. 9th November, 1816; suspensions amounting to $977.
Chambers, James, ensign	40.00	Advanced on account of pay of the army.
Campbell, John B. colonel	959.15	Balance on settlement, 9th February, 1815.
Carson, Charles, captain 15th	50.00	Advanced on account of bounties, &c.
Campbell, Robert, lieutenant 28th	150.00	Advanced on account of bounties, &c.
Clark, Robert, lieutenant 28th	550.00	Accounts rendered, without vouchers, for $82; leaving an apparent balance due of $468; states he has lost his vouchers.
Carson, Hugh H. lieutenant 10th	1,072.43	Balance on settlement, 2d April, 1814, $130.63, and advanced made him, subsequently, on account of quartermaster department, bounties, and contingencies.
Crooks, Robert B. lieutenant 28th	242.00	Advanced on account of bounties, &c.
Caldwell, Elias B. colonel dragoons	704.50	Advanced, on account of contingencies, for the purpose of erecting telegraphs; he has rendered accounts and vouchers, upon which he claims to be due him $427.45.
Chittenden, Giles G. contractor	186.75	Payment made by Jacob Brown, lieutenant 11th, for rations furnished his recruits, on failure of the contractor.
Chapman, Jeremiah, captain 9th	524.00	Balance on settlement, 28th February, 1816, $224; since brought to his debit, $300; supposed to have an account for pay.
Chittenden, Thomas, lieutenant 30th	540.00	Accounts rendered, without vouchers, for $340; leaving apparent balance of $200.

STATEMENT--Continued

Names and Rank	Amount Dolls.Cts.	Remarks
Coles, Issac A. colonel	108.90	Advanced him by Ferdinand Marsteller, on account of contingencies.
Cummings, James, ensign	50.00	Advanced him on account of bounties, &c.
Chase, Charles, captain volunteer cavalry	50.00	Advanced him on account of quartermaster department.
Cranson, John H. lieutenant 9th	30.00	Advanced him on account of the pay of the army.
Cromwell, John I. lieutenant 3d artillery	1,008.00	Accounts rendered, without vouchers, for $48; leaving an apparent balance of $200.
Cowan, Andrew, ensign	500.00	Advanced on account of bounties, &c.
Chappell, William, captain, 45th	632.00	Balance on settlement, 29th October, 1816; suspensions amounting to $98.0
Coles, Leonard, ensign 26th	66.80	Do. do. 4th February, 1820; suspensions amounting to $9.80.
Conner, Samuel S. lieutenant colonel 13th	7.51	Do. do. 9th August, 1814.

STATEMENT--Continued

Names and Rank	Amount Dolls.Cts.	Remarks
Callaway, Francis, lieutenant	330.00	Advanced on account of bounties and pay of the army.
Cole, John B. lieutenant 35th	54.50	Balance on settlement, 24th September, 1816; suspensions amounting to $52.
Crowder, Robert A. lieutenant 35th	290.46	Do. do. 27th February, 1817. He claims pay and emoluments to amount of $217.
Carr, Robert W. ensign 35th	833.00	Advanced on account of bounties, &c.
Charlton, Francis D. lieutenant 35th	70.55	Balance on settlement, 8th June, 1816.
Clinch, Joseph I. lieutenant 10th	174.00	Advanced on account of quartermaster department, and bounties, &c.
Carter, Charles L. Philadelphia	50.00	Advanced him on account of medical and hospital departments, for the procuring accommodations at Fredericksburg, Virginia, for the sick left by lieutenant colonel Hamilton.
Carr, Charles, Kentucky militia	39,884.37	Accounts under examination; has refunded the balance according to his own statement.
Cooper, Gabriel L. 46th regiment	48,063.45	Accounts and vouchers rendered, and under examination, by which the money appears to be nearly all accounted for.
Chandler, John, quartermaster Virginia militia	3,437.22	Advanced on account of militia.
Chaldwell, John, lieutenant	50.00	Advanced on account of bounties, &c.
Clark, John, ensign 22d	500.00	Accounts rendered for $72, without vouchers.
Clark, Charles, lieutenant artillery	114.63	Balance on settlement 27th September, 1815.
Claiborn, F. L. brigadier gen. Mississippi volunteers	200.00	Advanced on account of camp equipage, &c.
Collins, John, ensign 15th	182.00	Advanced on account of bounties, &c.
Crump, John G. lieutenant	100.00	Advanced on account of bounties, &c.
Coming, M. captain 11th	1,000.00	Advanced on account of contingencies.
Cummings, Calvin, ensign 21st	50.00	Advanced on account of contingencies.
Carroll, John, lieutenant 27th	400.00	Advanced on account of bounties, &c.
Clary, E. A. lieutenant 40th	57.75	Balance on settlement, 13th July, 1816.
Clark, Thomas, Philadelphia	13,000.00	Advanced him on account of fortifications at the Pea. Patch, Delaware. had rendered accounts and vouchers for $12,000.
Campbell, James, lieutenant 17th	487.44	Balance on settlement 16th November, 1816; suspensions amounting to $478.83 ½.
Carrington, Edward, captain	50.00	Advanced on account of hospital department.
Conner, Daniel, lieutenant 28th	40.41	Balance on settlement, 21st March, 1817.
Campbell, James, major 43d	245.09	Do. do. do. suspensions amounting to $120.
Campbell, James H. captain	289.35	Has a claim for pay, &c. which amounts to more than this balance.
Crawford, Obadiah, lieutenant	195.00	Advanced on account of pay, bounties, and contingencies.

STATEMENT--Continued

Names and Rank	Amount Dolls.Cts.	Remarks
Cook, Philip, major 8th	134.24	Balance on settlement, 20th May, 1818. Suspensions $3.75.
Clark, Waters, major 44th	379.00	Do. do. 5th June, 1818, $479. He has subsequently received credit for $100. Suspensions $83.
Canfield, L. B. captain, 23d	280.11	Do. do. 22d January, 1818; claims balance of $102.28; difference arising from suspensions including $33.59 for pay and subsistence.
Carr, Robert, major	667.39	Balance on settlement, 4th August, 1818; promises to refund balance.
Clendenin, Robert, late member of Congress	90.81	Do. do. 15th April, 1817, $73.88. He has since been charged $16.93 on account of medical and hospital department.

STATEMENT--Continued

Names and Rank	Amount Dolls.Cts.	Remarks
Camp, Thomas, assistant deputy quartermaster general	3,928.00	Balance on settlement, Dead. It is represented that he probably disbursed this money, but the accounts cannot be found.
Clark, Matthew, paymaster Kentucky militia	146.77	Balance on settlement, 16th May, 1820.
Craig, Robert H. lieutenant 2d dragoons	3,013.85	Do. do. 19th November, 1819. Reported for suit 24th November, 1819.
Coleman, Samuel, lieutenant 9th	466.90	Do. do. 14th May, 1817 Amount of suspensions greater than the balance.
Chilton, William, lieutenant 2d riflemen	126.00	Do. do. 16th July, 1819. Amount of suspensions more than the balance.
Chase, Moses I. lieutenant 3d	359.46	Do. do. 21 October, 1818. He only acknowledges a balance due U. S. of $169.49. Reported for suit 20th October, 1819.
Chapman, John, lieutenant 6th infantry	144.00	Balance on settlement, 23d May, 1817, $44; suspensions $94. Has had a subsequent advance of $70.
Clark, Nathan, lieutenant 37th	412.43	Do. do. 13th May, 1819. Suspensions $366.60.
Clark, Patterson B. ensign 2d riflemen	698.00	Do. do. 1st October, 1818. Reported for suit 20th October 1819.
Chapman, Matthew, lieutenant 3d	218.00	Advanced on account of bounties, &c.
Chunn, John T. brigade major	985.00	Accounts rendered for $635.52 without vouchers, but a small part of which are admissible. Promises to render his accounts and vouchers.
Cushing, Daniel, captain 2d	3,122.39	Balance on settlement, 24th February, 1820. Suspensions $170.
Cissna, Charles	109.75	Do. do. 6th August, 1817.
Cornyn, Dominick, lieutenant 22d	2,750.00	Advanced on account of bounties and contingencies.
Corcoran, Thomas, captain, 36th	758.75	Balance on settlement 6th March, 1820. Suspensions $14. Has a claim for pay, &c.
Chrystie, John, lieutenant colonel	598.30	Balance on settlement 25th August, 1820.
Charlton, James, captain, 12th	1,638.45	Do. do. 14th March, 1820. Reported for suit 23d September, 1819.
Craig, James, lieutenant 21st	209.66	Do. do. 26th August, 1817. Suspensions $136.90
Clough, Moses, lieutenant 34th	978.24	Advanced on account of bounties and contingencies. Settlement 4th January 1817, $405.30 suspended.
Carter, Isaac, captain 34th	1,815.23	Balance on settlement 17th September, 1817. Suspensions $888.67. Reported for suit 28th September, 1820.
Cass, Lewis B. general	3,000.00	Do. do. 7th May, 1815. Advanced on account of contingencies for the recruiting service.

STATEMENT--Continued

Names and Rank	Amount Dolls.Cts.	Remarks
Chaffee, John, paymaster	8.49	Do. do. 12th August, 1812.
Childs, Rudolphus R. lieutenant 30th	.41	Do. do. 9th January, 1818.
Campbell, Thomas I.	8,000.00	Advanced on account of quartermaster department.
Childs, Thomas, lieutenant	117.58	Balance on settlement 22d January, 1818.
Cooper, Enoch, lieutenant 11th	252.00	Do. do. 9th February, 1818
Craig, Henry K. captain artillery	95.13	Do. do. 30th November, 1819.
Carty, Josiah S. lieutenant 42d	300.00	Advanced on account of contingencies.
Conant, Augustus F. lieutenant 29th	130.06	Balance on settlement, 8th June, 1820. Suspensions to this amount.
Claiborne, William C. C. governor of Louisiana	5,000.00	Advanced on account of pay of the militia of Louisiana; doubtless it has been applied, but no account rendered.
Cummings, Francis D. captain	172.00	Balance on settlement 23d March, 1820. Suspensions $4.
Callan, Patrick lieutenant 2d dragoons	3.00	Accounts rendered, claims a balance.

STATEMENT--Continued

Names and Rank	Amount Dolls.Cts.	Remarks
Chaflin, Elliot, ensign 9th infantry	634.23	Accounts rendered without vouchers for $291.98, leaving an apparent balance of $342.25.
Calvin, Robert B. paymaster	12.00	Balance on settlement, 25th July, 1818.
Cass, Charles L lieutenant 19th	207.00	do. do. 13th April, 1818. Suspensions $128.13.
Cantine, Moses C. lieutenant 13th	1,846.00	do. do. 7th March, 1820. Reported for suit 7th September, 1820.
Cook, Hamlin, deputy paymaster	69,382.66	do. do. 15th May, 1820. He is entitled to credit $482. He will be entitled to credits to a large amount on removing objections and furnishing additional vouchers. Reported for suit.
Connelly, John M. captain 3d artillery	514.55	do. do. 7th April, 1820. Suspensions $181.27.
Chaplin, James, late paymaster col. Wood's reg. Va. Militia	5,125.34	do. do. 1st March, 1817.
Carleton, Jonathan, paymaster Ohio militia	76,263.80	No accounts rendered. Written to on the subject of his accounts 5th August, 1817. Reported for suit.
Clark, Salmon, captain 30th	975.00	Accounts rendered without vouchers for $230, leaving an apparent balance of $745.
Cox, Levi	341.25	Balance on settlement, 5th October, 1820. Reported for suit.
Church, Thomas M. lieutenant 16th	139.41	do. do. 18th June, 1818. Suspensions equal to this amount.
Cooper, John B. deputy paymaster	17,962.47	do. do. 23d August, 1820. Suspensions $16,927.43.
Claiborne, M. M. ensign 12th	178.00	Advanced on account of bounties and contingencies.
Campbell, Henry M. lieutenant 2d artillery	49.00	Advanced on account of quartermaster department and contingencies.
Conkey, Joshua, captain New York Volunteers	135.00	Balance on settlement, 10th July, 1818, $125, and has subsequently been charged with $10.
Coffee, William, lieutenant 15th	676.00	Advanced on account of quartermaster department and volunteers.
Campbell, Thomas, captain and ass. Dep. Q.M. Gen.	6,183.50	Balance on settlement, 24th July, 1818. Suspensions of $55. Reported for suit 20th September, 1819.
Carroll, William, general	1,586.32	do. do. 25th July, 1818. Suspensions, $1,329.15.
Campbell, John, captain 13th	198.71	do. do. 25th July, 1818.
Canty, Charles, lieutenant 43d	244.00	do. do. 6th August, 1818. Suspensions $133.95.
Cockran, Andrew P captain, 45th	16.00	do. do. 8th August, 1818.
Campbell, John, captain, 26th	3,190.00	Advanced on account of bounties, &c.
Cooke, Giles B. Virginia militia	150,692.84	Accounts and vouchers rendered. Balanced, per his statement; under examination.
Clark, Joshua, paymaster Georgia militia	3,875.22	Balance on settlement, 21 April, 1820. Suspensions $3,860. 8.

STATEMENT--Continued

Names and Rank	Amount Dolls.Cts.	Remarks
Cutler, Enos, major 2d infantry	279.25	do. do. 9th September, 1818. Suspensions $218.25.
Crawford, William M. lieutenant 24th	88.25	do. do. 16th October, 1819.
Coleman, Samuel, ensign 8th infantry	200.00	Advanced him on account of bounties, &c.
Conrad, Samuel, paymaster Pennsylvania militia	777.70	Balance on settlement, 7th December, 1818. Suspensions $29.16. Reported for suit 28th October, 1820.
Cadwallader, Isaac, paymaster Penns. Volunteers	1,280.01	do. do. 26th November, 1818. Suspensions $798.24. Reported for suit 3d October, 1820.
Callis, O. W. lieutenant	281.50	Accounts and vouchers rendered, upon which he claims a balance; but he acknowledges to have received other funds, which is not embraced in his accounts rendered. A settlement awaits the rendition of the accounts of colonel Preston.
Cohen, Hyem, lieutenant riflemen	360.00	Advanced him on account of bounties, &c.
Cox, Jonathan, ensign 12th	25.91	Balance on settlement, 30th December, 1818.

Names and Rank	Amount Dolls.Cts.	Remarks
Clemson, Eli B. captain 1st infantry	271.76	Balance on settlement, 17th May, 1819.
Clement, John, paymaster Elmore's brig. N. J. militia	644.05	do. do. 6th March, 1819.
Carpenter, Isaac, lieutenant 40th	987.21	Account rendered, claims credit for the amount here charged; but has rendered no vouchers.
Counsilman, Jacob, paymaster 36th Maryland militia	216.02	Balance on settlement, 8th February, 1819. Suspensions $161.56.
Covington, William A. lieutenant 39th	496.00	do. do. 10th February, 1819.
Cummings, David, captain 14th	460.00	do. do. 24th February, 1819. Has claims to this amount for bounties and premiums, the vouchers for which he states to have delivered to the colonel of the regiment, and which cannot now be found, but which he is preparing otherwise to establish.
Carey, John P. late paymaster Georgia militia	2,104.06	do. do. 18th March, 1819. Suspensions $1840.24.
Cowan, David G. lieutenant 28th	723.50	do. do. 15th October, 1819. Suspensions $112.
Chambers, Talbot, lieutenant colonel riflemen	550.50	Advanced on account of bounties &c.; states he has lost his papers.
Call, Robert, ensign 12th	40.46	Balance on settlement, 6th July, 1820.
Clark, Joseph, lieutenant 28th	500.00	Advanced on account of bounties, &c.
Chilton, George W. paymaster 16th Kentucky militia	306.72	Balance on settlement, 29th June, 1819.
Clay, Joseph, captain, 10th	873.28	do. do. 17th May, 1819. Suspensions $22, and reported for suit 27th September, 1819.
Creel, David, paymaster Virginia militia		do. do. 22 April, 1820, Settled 16th November, 1820: Balance refunded.
Creed, Wilson, ensign 7th	22.00	do. do. 19th May, 1819.
Coombs, R. L. lieutenant 43d	550.00	No accounts or vouchers rendered.
Carr, Francis, ensign 21st	348.49	Balance on settlement, 8th June, 1819.
Carrick Addison, last assist. dep. quartermast. gen	5,392.79	Balance on settlement, 1st July, 1819. Suspensions amounting to $3011.47, for want of proper vouchers. Reported for suit, 8th July, 1819.
Clark, Abraham, lieutenant, 14th infantry	19.41	Balance on settlement, 17th July, 1819. Suspensions $20.
Cox, John P. paymaster New York militia	3,879.95	Do do 29th April, 1820. States that he has no further accounts to render.
Currin, William captain Virginia militia	11.11	Do do 2d February, 1820
Crabb, Richard I. captain 14th	132.00	Do do 8th July, 1819. Suspensions $8.
Champlain, Samuel, deputy paymaster, &c.	141,251.03	Do do 15h July, 1819. Reported for suit, 26th July, 1819.
Campbell, James H. captain 24th	289.35	Advanced on account of bounties, &c.

STATEMENT--Continued

Names and Rank	Amount Dolls.Cts.	Remarks
Clark, James, member of Congress	280.71	Balance on settlement, 6th November, 1819. Suspensions $159.50.
Clarkson, Charles S. assistant deputy paymaster	2,431.31	Do do 15th June, 1820. Suspensions $1030.31.
Coleman, Joseph, deputy paymaster, deceased	281,196.85	Accounts and vouchers in part rendered; apparent balance of $160,808.53; states he has further accounts to render which will cover this balance. He is now dead, and his accounts and vouchers, which are very voluminous, are preparing for suit.
Colbert, James, Indian chief	14,133.55	Advanced by the paymaster general on account of the pay, subsistence, and clothing, of the Chickasaw Indians, in the service of the United States, in 1814.
Clark, William to pay Virginia militia	3,334.85	Advanced on account of the pay of the army.

STATEMENT--Continued

Names and Rank	Amount Dolls.Cts.	Remarks
Curtis, William H. lieutenant 12th	215.00	Advanced on account of bounties, &c.
Campbell, William, captain light artillery	2,718.26	Advanced on account of bounties and contingencies. Suspensions on Settlement, 15th July, 1816, $1,148.21.
Cocks, William, captain artillery	78.00	Balance on settlement, 17th September, 1819. Claims a balance.
Campbell, John, lieutenant colonel 28th	2,353.87	Do do 17th do 1819. Reported for suit, 28 September, 1820.
Clark, John G. lieutenant 5th	76.00	Advanced on account of pay and contingencies.
Conkling, Frederick, lieutenant 4th	1,369.75	Balance on settlement, 29th October, 1819. Reported for suit, 10th November, 1819.
Cone, Festus, captain	122.00	Advanced on account of bounties, &c.
Cutter, Jacob, assistant deputy paymaster	355.48	Balance on settlement, 30th October, 1820. Suspensions $272.33.
Caldwell, Richard, lieutenant	430.00	Advanced on account of bounties, &c.
Clark, Satterlee, district paymaster	8,468.95	Balance on settlement, 3d November, 1820. Has additional accounts to render, which he states will meet this balance.
Cuyler, Ralph B. lieutenant 6th	1,562.36	Balance on settlement, 30th October, 1819. Reported for suit 10th November, 1819
Cloud, George, captain 10th	883.47	Do do 23rd December, 1819. Suspensions, $155.50
Caruthers, Madison, paymaster 5th Virginia militia	183.76	Balance on settlement, 29th December, 1819. Suspensions amounting to $53.33, requiring additional evidence.
Collins, Thomas, late captain volunteers	2,000.00	Balance on settlement, 11th November, 1819. Reported for suit, 24th November, 1819. Has rendered an account, and vouchers for $1,352.97.
Cross, Hoverton, lieutenant 42d	220.00	No accounts rendered.
Duffell, Henry L. lieutenant 12th	19.59	Balance on settlement, 28th October, 1816.
Delano, Alnasa D. paymaster,	606.84	Advanced on account of militia.
Deyo, Henry, ensign, 13th	73.58	Balance on settlement, 25th September, 1820. Suspensions $8.
Dunlap, James, major Pennsylvania militia	300.00	Advanced on account of militia
Davenport, William, captain 16th	514.20	Balance on settlement, 26th July, 1820
Dixon, Don C. lieutenant and paymaster 24th	155.46	Advanced on account of pay, subsistence and forage.
Delong, Samuel	176.00	Balance on settlement, 2d September, 1820. Reported for suit 26th September, 1820.
Dearborne, Simon, lieutenant 34th	505.15	Do do 14th November, 1816. Suspensions $422.11.
Davis, Peter, lieutenant 28th	788. 3	Advanced on account of bounties and pay of the army.
Dubois, John captain sea fencibles	1,500.00	Accounts rendered without vouchers, on which he claims a balance.

STATEMENT--Continued

Names and Rank	Amount Dolls.Cts.	Remarks
Dearborne, Thomas, lieutenant 33d	81.60	Accounts rendered without vouchers for $80, leaving an apparent balance, of $1.60.
Drew, Francis, captain, 33d	6.00	Balance on settlement, 24th November, 1815, and 23d January, 1816.
Dennison, William ensign volunteers	125.00	Advanced on account of pay of the army.
Davis, Isaac, surgeon 6th infantry	25.60	Advanced on account of contingencies.
David John T. paymaster 15th	29,003.55	Balance on settlement, 27th April 1814, $390.75. Do. on settlement 31 January 1815, $4,769.54 and on settlement 15th February, 1815, $23,843.26. He states his vouchers to have been destroyed by fire, and has petitioned Congress for relief.

STATEMENT--Continued

Names and Rank	Amount Dolls.Cts.	Remarks
Donnelly, Petr, lieutenant 13th	64.00	Advanced on account of bounties, &c.
Dwight, Joseph H. ensign 13th	334.39	Balance on settlement, 9th May and 19th July, 1814.
Davis, Isaac, lieutenant 2d artillery	280.00	Advanced on account of bounties and contingencies.
Dyer, Otis, lieutenant, 8th	364.79	Balance on settlement, 2d May, 1816.
Daniels, Charles, lieutenant 35th	58.98	Advanced on account of contingencies, for the transportation of his baggage from Washington city to Louis.
Darnell, John, lieutenant 2d infantry	64.80	Advanced on account of quartermaster department.
Downes, Richard C. surgeon's mate 14th	5.00	Advanced on account of contingencies.
Davidge, Thomas, ensign	150.00	Advanced on account of contingencies.
Dennison, Washington, ensign	220.00	Advanced on account of pay of the army.
Dobbin, H. W. lieutenant colonel militia	174.22	Advanced on account of subsistence.
Dickinson, Silas, captain, 31st	748.56	Balance on settlement 17th Feb. 1817. Suspensions amounting to $412.80, requiring additional vouchers.
Dodge, Richard, brigadier general	231.20	Advanced on account of militia.
Denny, Thomas, cadet	150.00	Advanced on account of contingencies.
Darby, Benjamin, lieutenant 30th	109.22	Balance on settlement 18th September, 1816.
Dupey, Antoine, paymaster 44th regiment	61,417.93	Accounts on file and under examination.
Daggett, Thomas, lieutenant 2d	600.00	Advanced him on account of bounties, &c.
Doherty, John, lieutenant militia cavalry	470.00	Advanced on account of quartermaster department.
Dyer, William M. ensign 9th	241.89	Balance on settlement, 28th January, 1820. Suspensions $61.20.
Duncan, Samuel, A. D. quartermaster general	350.74	Advanced on account of quartermaster department.
Downs, John, lieutenant 21st	200.00	Advanced on account of bounties, &c.
Derby, Benjamin, captain	50.00	Advanced on account of bounties, &c.
Dounes, Jeremiah, captain rifle militia	10.27	Balance on settlement 9th April, 1816.
Dixey, John T. lieutenant 40th	20.00	Advanced on account of contingencies.
Deman, Jeremiah, lieutenant	165.00	Advanced on account of bounties, &c.
Doyle, Richard, lieutenant 17th	128.13	Balance on settlement 7th April, 1820. Suspensions to a greater amount that this balance.
Dudley, I. captain, 28th	200.00	Advanced on account of bounties, &c.
Dupey, Gaspard, lieutenant 44th	372.00	Advance don account of bounties, &c.
Danielson, F. E. ensign 19th	29.00	Advanced on account of contingencies.
Duncan, Benjamin, lieuteuant 39th	10.00	Advanced on account of contingencies.
Duane, William colonel	4,317.74	Balance on settlement, 1st October, 1819. Reported for suit 5th October, 1819. States that he has additional claims.

STATEMENT--Continued

Names and Rank	Amount Dolls.Cts.	Remarks
Dunham, George, ensign 33rd	228.00	Account rendered for $245.49, only 108.35 of which being supported by vouchers.
Durant, Charles, lieutenant 40th	143.68	Balance on settlement 21st April, 1817. Suspensions to amount of 108.35 of which being supported by vouchers.
Dyson, Samuel T. captain	1,442.13	Do do 7th July, 1820.
Dearing, James H. lieutenant artillery	294.77	Do do 21st July, 1817. Suspensions of $60.

Names and Rank	Amount Dolls.Cts.	Remarks
Desha, Benjamin, captain 2d riflemen	135.98	Balance on settlement, 21 August, 1817. Suspensions $114.
Dortch, Norft. Lieutenant 39th	445.09	Do do 28th May, 1817.
Dawson, Joseph, ensign 28th	16.94	Do do 1st December, 1817.
Dinsmore, Silas, Indian agent	80.00	Advanced on account of quartermaster department.
Darrington, John, colonel 4th infantry	642.62	Balance on settlement 1st June, 1817.
Dick, E. D.	1,830.58	Do do 5th January, 1819. Suspensions, $1,436.48.
Dewey, Samuel M. captain	463.72	Do so 29th October, 1819. Reported for suit 10th November, 1819.
Dix, Timothy, major	13,114.14	Accounts rendered without vouchers for $960 leaving an apparent balance of $12,154.14. Died in service. Has accounts to render for disbursements.
Dana, Daniel, colonel 31st	4,198.48	Balance on settlement 13th January, 1820. Says he intends to petition Congress.
Dent, Lewis, paymaster	603.24	Do do 1st November, 1819. Reported for suit 2d November, 1819.
Davis, William W. lieutenant	286.75	Do do 1st October, 1817. Suspensions of $66.47.
Dunn, Benjamin captain	280.25	Advanced on account of bounties and pay of the army.
Deneale, Hugh W. captain, 36th	683.50	Balance on settlement 23d June, 1818. Suspensions $113.50. Reported for suit 27th Sept. 1820.
Dorman, James, major	400.00	Advanced on account of quartermaster department, bounties, and contingencies.
Danvers, Matthew D. captain 29th	4,537.03	Balance on settlement, 10th September, 1817. Suspensions $4.
Dade, Francis L. lieutenant 12th	5.16	Advanced on account of bounties, &c.
Darrow, Daniel M. lieutenant 27th	142.00	Balance on settlement 16th September, 1817. Suspensions equal to this balance.
Dobbin, Archibald, assistant deputy paymaster	26,122.25	Balance on settlement 30th October, 1820. Suspensions $498.13. Reported for suit. Has further accounts to render.
Davis, John M. assistant inspector general	400.00	Advanced on account of quartermaster department.
Dubois, I. L.	4,940.00	Accounts rendered without vouchers for $240, leaving an apparent balance of $4,700.
Denton, Thomas W. lieutenant 13th	100.00	Advanced on account of bounties, &c.
Donaldson, Stephen F. paymaster 14th	16,442.87	Balance on settlement 12th July, 1820. Suspensions $52.04. Reported for suit 3d October, 1820.
Davis, John, captain	208.50	Advanced on account of bounties and contingencies.
De Peyster, William, lieutenant	100.00	Balance on settlement, 19th March, 1819.

STATEMENT--Continued

Names and Rank	Amount Dolls.Cts.	Remarks
Doussett, Augustus, ensign 8th	8.20	Do do 27th January, 1820.
Duncan, Joseph, lieutenant 17th	1,290.00	Accounts rendered, without vouchers, for $478.26; leaving an apparent balance due, $811.74.
Dawson, Nicholas L. paymaster Md. Militia	7,363.21	Balance on settlement, 3d September, 1819. Reported for suit, 17 June, 1818.
Doane, David, captain, 45th	34.00	Do do 26th June, 1818. Suspensions, $4.
Dickerson, Jacob, ensign 15th	578.05	Do do 1st September, 1818.
Dunckel, George F.	1,400.00	Advanced on account of quartermaster department.
Davis, E. L. lieutenant	27.00	Advanced on account of quartermaster department.
Davis, Samuel B. lieutenant colonel 32d	1,306.00	Balance on settlement, 9th November, 1819. and reported for suit, 24th November, 1819.
Davis, Aquilla, colonel volunteers	500.00	Advanced on account of quartermaster department.

STATEMENT--Continued

Names and Rank	Amount Dolls.Cts.	Remarks
Dinkins, James E. major	328.39	Balance on settlement, 8th July, 1819.
Dearing, Anthony, ensign 39th	1,500.00	Do do 29th August, 1818. Suspensions, $186. Reported for suit, 27th September, 1820.
Dennis, Richard, colonel 18th	24,840.18	Do do 1st June, 1820. Reported for suit, 22 July, 1820.
Diffenback, Lewis, ensign 18th	116.00	Accounts rendered for $43; vouchers support $20 only; leaving an apparent balance of $73.
Davis, H. H. captain 32d	239.00	Advanced on account of bounties and contingencies.
Donaldson, John, jun. acting paymaster Penn. Militia	670.04	Balance on settlement, 6th November, 1818. Reported for suit, 3d October, 1820.
Delovac, Alexander, lieutenant 26th	726.00	Advanced on account of bounties and contingencies.
Douglass, Thompson, deputy paymaster	28,080.57	Balance on settlement, 8th October, 1819. Suspensions, $13,603.98. Reported for suit, 13th Jan. 1820.
Duncan, Thomas, paymaster Penn. Militia	93.52	Do do 16th February, 1819.
Drew, Ira, lieutenant	568.71	Do do 11th August, 1819. Suspensions, $104.66.
Deardorff, Christian, paymaster 3d Ohio militia	24.00	Do do 6th March, 1819.
Denton, Joel, lieutenant, 39th	344.47	Do do 18th March, 1819, $501.47. Suspensions $280. 4. He has refunded to the Paymaster general $157; leaving a balance against him of $344.47.
Dawes, James, paymaster 27th Maryland militia	385.70	Do do 19th March, 1819.
Davis, James, captain, 39th	2,322.00	Do do 21st December, 1819. Suspensions, $62. Reported for suit, 28th September, 1820
Doherty, William, lieutenant 2d rifle	535.84	Do do 30th April, 1819. Suspensions $31.12 ½.
Dunham, Lewis, surgeon	4.92	Do do 16th October, 1819.
Duncan, James, captain, 17th	1,610.00	Accounts rendered amounting to nearly the balance against him. He states he will refund the balance when ascertained.
Doherty, James, major 28th	121.24	Balance on settlement, 18th May, 1819. Suspensions for want of proper vouchers, $109.
Durant, Jackson, lieutenant 4th	221.71	Do do 18th May, 1819.
Duncan, William R. captain artillery	98.00	Do do 1st June, 1819.
Duncan, John, ensign 21st	77.34	Do do 29th August, 1820
Desha, Robert, major 24th	312.99	Do do 23rd October, 1820. Suspensions, $91.50
Dunn, William, paymaster 35th	13,163.34	Accounts and vouchers rendered, upon which he claims a balance.
Draper, Henry, ensign 9th	32.00	Accounts rendered; no vouchers; acknowledges a balance due of $10.
Dumbleton, George, lieutenant 29th	1,768.52	Advanced on account of bounties, &c.

STATEMENT--Continued

Names and Rank	Amount Dolls.Cts.	Remarks
Dunlap, William, assistant deputy paymaster	24,432.50	Accounts rendered and under examination.
Douglass, Alfred H. captain 39th	168.70	Balance on settlement, 6th November, 1819. Suspensions $137.
Dudley, Ambrose, paymaster Kentucky militia	1,048. 3	Do do 31st December, 1819. Suspensions, $1051.59.
Edes, Jeremiah, lieutenant 34th	1,093.82	Do do 4th January, 1817. Suspensions, $186.42.
Eddy, Farley, lieutenant	.24	Advanced on account of bounties &c.
Emmery, Jeremiah, jun. captain, 33d	199.65	Balance on settlement, 5th January, 1810. Suspensions equal to this balance.
Eastman, Jonathan B. deputy paymaster	62,774.17	Do do 20th May, 1814. Act passed for his relief, but his statements and evidences are so unsatisfactory as to make it impracticable with them to make a statement.

STATEMENT--Continued

Names and Rank	Amount Dolls.Cts.	Remarks
Elliott, James, captain 3d artillery	499.50	Advanced on account of bounties and contingencies.
Edney, John M lieutenant colonel 10th	1,000.00	Advanced on account of quartermaster department.
Edmonson, Thomas, lieutenant 28th	58.00	Advanced on account of bounties, &c.
Emigh, Nicholas, captain militia	50.00	Advanced on account of quartermaster department.
Eddy, Tisdale, major	175.00	Advanced on account of quartermaster department.
Everest, Calvin, lieutenant	150.00	Advanced on account of pay of the army.
Eddy, Jonathan, lieutenant 31st	274.31	Balance on settlement, 18th July, 1815
Easton, Thomas, quartermaster militia	36.20	Do do 9th April, 1816.
Eubank, William, lieutenant 17th	390.00	Advanced on account of pay, bounties, and contingencies.
Evans, A. ensign 17th	190.00	Advanced on account of pay, bounties, and contingencies.
Evans, Henry F.	1,550.00	Advanced on account of quartermaster department and bounties, &c.
Emmons, Elisha, lieutenant 31st	216.02	Balance on settlement, 1st June, 1818. Suspensions amounting to $214.32, requiring vouchers.
Ewing, John	.15	Do. do. 23d February, 1820.
Eakin, Samuel H. deputy paymaster,	1,406,132.74	Accounts and vouchers rendered, and in course of settlement.
Earle, Samuel G. captain 43d	369.94	Balance on settlement, 20th December, 1817. Suspensions $44.
Eastman, Jonathan, paymaster 21st	735.01	Do. do. 13th October, 1818.
Edmonds, Samuel, paymaster general N. Y. militia	563,337.76	Accounts and vouchers rendered, and in course of settlement.
Evans, Henry H. paymaster Ohio militia	2,688.46	Balance on settlement, 27th December, 1919. Suspensions $12.48.
Eustis, Abraham, lieutenant colonel artillery	192.03	Do. do. 5th May, 1820
Easter, Richard I. lieutenant paymaster 8th inf.	1,070.45	Do. do. 20th January, 1820. Has additional claims for $418.53, which requires further vouchers.
Eckfieldt, George, lieutenant 16th	540.00	Balance on settlement, 5th September, 1820.
Edmondson, William, lieutenant, 43d	61.50	Do. do. 4th June, 1818. Suspensions, $8.
Evans, Thomas, ensign, 16th	64.05	Do. do. 20th July, 1820. Suspensions $35.62.
Earle, William N. lieutenant 36th	299.83	Do. do. 11th July, 1818. Suspensions $50. Reported for suit, 26th September, 1820.
Egerton, Lebbons	7.13	Do. do. 16th May, 1820. Suspensions $6.
Edgcomb, Nicholas, lieutenant 33d	42.00	Do. do. 16th October, 1818. Suspensions $58.00.
Elliott, Wilson, captain 19th	576.00	He acknowledges other moneys, in addition to the sum here charged, leaving the balance against him $944.
Epes, Richard, paymaster 4th Virginia militia	255.77	Balance on settlement, 2d May, 1820. Will be entitled to further credits, when the objects to suspensions are removed.
Elmore, Benjamin T captain	45.59	Balance on settlement, 28th July, 1820. Suspensions $2.

STATEMENT--Continued

Names and Rank	Amount Dolls.Cts.	Remarks
Edsal, Richard, lieutenant 15th	19.00	Do. do. 27th February, 1819. Suspensions $12.
Eskridge, George ensign 15th	100.00	Do. do. 19th August, 1819. Suspensions, $4.33.
Edwards, Robert, captain, 17th	100.00	Advanced on account of contingencies.
Erb, John, paymaster Pennsylvania militia	1,164.63	Balance on settlement, 16th October, 1820.

STATEMENT--Continued

Names and Rank	Amount Dolls.Cts.	Remarks
Estis, William, paymaster 4th Virginia militia	5,223.59	Balance on settlement, 2d February, 1820. He will be entitled to further credits on suspended vouchers.
Eddy, Russell, lieutenant and paymaster 25th	160.51	Advanced on account of pay and forage.
Evans, John T. issuing commissary N. W. army	7,484.55	Advanced on account of militia, being provision to be issued.
Everett, John F. lieutenant 3d infantry	6,587.95	Balance on settlement, 27th September, 1819. Reported for suit, 5th October, 1819.
Eubank, James T. assistant deputy quartermaster	12,228.62	Balance on settlement, 30th September, 1819. Reported for suit, 5th October, 1819.
Ellis, Solomon , late contractor	12,375.13	Do. do. do. do.
Evans, George W. late quartermaster general	1,582.72	Reported for suit, 29th October, 1819. Suspensions on settlement, August, 1814. $750.
Furgusson, George W. lieutenant 22d	605.60	Balance on settlement, 2d September, 1820. Reported for suit, 26th September, 1820.
Fulton, Robert, contractor for steam boats	40,000.00	Do. do. 7th October, 1820. Reported for suit, 10th October, 1820.
Fairfax, Ferdinand	70.00	Do. do. 4th August, 1820.
Foote, David, ensign 9th	493.80	Do. do. 13th September, 1816, $469.80, and $24 advanced him on account of pay of the army. Suspensions $188.
French, Thomas, lieutenant 25th	846.00	Balance on settlement, 4th May, 1820.
Fannin, Jepthath, paymaster Georgia militia	2,289.39	Do. do. 9th February, 1820. Reported for suit, 3d October, 1820.
Floyd, David, assistant deputy quartermaster general	40.37	Advanced on account of militia.
Fousard, Daniel, lieutenant 25th	803.00	Advanced on account of pay, bounties, and contingencies.
Finch, Isaac, lieutenant	978.00	Balance on settlement, 19th July, 1820. States that Captain McElroy has his papers.
Findley, John	160.01	Do. do. 12th January, 1814. Suspensions $40.
Frasher, John, lieutenant, 29th	103.51	Do. do. 17th January, 1814.
Furman, John, lieutenant volunteers	185.00	Do. do. 2d September, 1820. Reported for suit, 26th September, 1820.
Farnsworth, Amos, surgeon's mate	50.00	Advanced on account of contingencies.
Fenwick, John R. colonel	3,630.00	He states he has vouchers to render.

STATEMENT--Continued

Names and Rank	Amount Dolls.Cts.	Remarks
Frazer, Donald, lieut. 15h & assis. Dep. paymaster	1,486.00	Vouchers rendered for $26.85 for recruiting purposes. He has also rendered his accounts as assistant deputy paymaster, upon upon which he acknowledges a balance of $297.30. vouchers stated to have been lost. Legislative interference necessary.
Fishbrown, William S. paymaster militia	234.75	Balance on settlement, 22d December, 1819.
Faulker, James, major artillery	70.00	Advanced on account of ordnance.
Fifield, Edward, lieutenant colonial militia	270.00	Advanced on account of contingencies.
Frederick, Henry, lieutenant 19th	140.66	Advanced on account of pay of the army.
Fowler, William, quartermaster New York militia	118.24	Balance on settlement, 12th December, 1814.
Finley, Thomas P. lieutenant and paymaster	8,390.07	Do. do. 9th May, 1814.
Fisher, Philip, ensign, 36th	46.00	Do. do. 17th June, 1814. He has a claim for $32.
Fenton, James, colonel	59.02	Do. do. October, 1820.
Farnum, Bradbury, lieutenant 21st	11.87	Balance on settlement, 2d August 1815.
Frisbee, G. captain New York volunteers	150.00	Advanced on account of quartermaster department.

Names and Rank	Amount Dolls.Cts.	Remarks
Farley, Henry F. ensign 35th	264.75	Vouchers for $222.75 rendered and on file for examination.
Farnham, Charles, lieutenant 4th	100.00	Advanced on account of bounties, &c.
Fullington, James	25.00	Advanced on account of quartermaster department.
Foster, William B. deputy commissary	1,049.58	Balance on settlement, 6th July, 1815
Fowler, Jacob, assistant deputy quartermaster general	176.04	Balance on settlement, 15th January, 1816. $289.10. He has subsequently received a credit, by James Morrison, for $133. 6, leaving him indebted to the United States $176. 4.
Fleehier, E. De. Quartermaster 44th	400.00	Advanced on account of contingencies.
Farriott, I. P. lieutenant 24th	776.00	Advanced on account of bounties, &c.
Fleming, John D. lieutenant	460.63	Balance on settlement, 2d December, 1819. Suspensions $17.53.
Ford, Patrick, lieutenant	131.10	Balance on settlement, 2d June, 1815, $108.14. He has subsequently been charged with $22.96, on account of contingencies; making the sum of $131.10 against him.
Freeman, Nehemiah D. paymaster	1,051,609.97	Accounts and vouchers rendered, and apparent balance $348.59. Not yet examined.
Fairchild, William H. lieutenant 43d	320.83	Balance on settlement, 2d March, 1820.
Findley, Thomas, lieutenant 16th	300.00	Advanced on account of bounties and contingencies.
Freeman, T. W. lieutenant artillery	152.33	Balance on settlement, 15th May, 1818. Has rendered additional Accounts and vouchers, and a balance appears in his favor.
Fishback, Martin, lieutenant 5th	2,104.00	Balance on settlement, 21st September, 1820. Reported for suit, 28th September, 1820
Farrington, Daniel, captain 30th	20.68	Balance on settlement, 4th April, 1818. Suspensions $73.
Fontaine, John I. lieutenant 2d artillery	55.00	Advanced on account of bounties, &c.
Farnsworth, Drummond, ensign 34th	318.01	Balance on settlement, 19th January, 1819. Suspensions $22.
Foster, William L. captain 9th	40.00	Advanced on account of bounties and contingencies.
Fuller, Charles, captain 4th	8.00	Balance on settlement, 10th November, 1817.
Fanning, Abraham, B. deputy quartermaster general	47,009.69	This is a charge brought to his debit for provisions received from the contractor, the disposition of which has not satisfactorily established. His account is not settled.
Foster, Edmund, captain 9th	945.00	Balance on settlement, 27th November, 1817. Suspensions $246.
Forsythe, Benjamin, captain riflemen, deceased	4,102.77	Accounts and vouchers rendered, and an apparent balance due him.
Fleming, Davis, captain, 3d artillery	2,250.00	Advanced on account of bounties, contingencies, and quartermaster department.
Finney, Herman, captain, 23d	188.79	Balance on settlement, 25th April, 1820. Additional accounts rendered.

STATEMENT--Continued

Names and Rank	Amount Dolls.Cts.	Remarks
Forbes, Caleb J. lieutenant 24th	1,126.06	Balance on settlement, 28th January, 1818. Suspensions $232.
French, Cornelius R. doctor	65.00	Advanced on account of quartermaster and hospital departments.
Fetter, Jacob, lieutenant 22d	600.00	Accounts rendered for $546.55, without vouchers.
Fields, Elisha, captain 4th	539.85	Balance on settlement, 12th April, 1818. Suspensions $326.85
Farwell, Abel, lieutenant, 11th	343.40	Balance on settlement, 27th April, 1818. Suspensions $573.68
Flanders, Joseph, captain 45th	8.00	Balance on settlement, 11th June, 1818. Suspensions, $8.
Fenk, John L. lieutenant 13th	800.00	Advanced on account of contingencies $100; received of John Chrystie $700; making $800.

STATEMENT--Continued

Names and Rank	Amount Dolls.Cts.	Remarks
Fendall, John, late lieutenant 5th	218.24	Balance on settlement, 27th May, 1818, $438.32. He has subsequently refunded $220. 8; leaving the balance of $218.24 against him. suspensions on the settlement $147.77.
Fenner, Robert, captain,	482.57	Balance on settlement, 2d September, 1818. Suspensions $151.62.
Fullerton, David, paymaster Pennsylvania volunteers	194.91	Balance on settlement, 24th August, 1818.
Fatherston, William ensign 17th	1,083.03	Balance on settlement, 9th June, 1818. Suspensions $382. 3.
Fox, Arthur, lieutenant 10th	233.84	Balance on settlement, 4th September, 1820. Reported for suit 26th September, 1820.
Flannagan, John, paymaster Pennsylvania volunteers,	578.41	No account rendered.
Farwell, John, lieutenant, 31st	510.00	Advanced on account of bounties and contingencies.
Farrar, Thomas W. captain 10th	140.71	Balance on settlement, 3d July, 1818, $156.71; has subsequently refunded $25; leaving $140.71 against him.
Farrow, John W. paymaster 18th	2,498.13	Balance on settlement, 29th June, 1820.
Fasset, Elias colonel 30th	5,047.25	Balance on settlement, 9th June, 1819, $3,047.25; suspensions $305.89; $2,000 since received of Walter Sheldon; making the balance.
Foster, Charles, ensign 9th	321.00	Balance on settlement, 8th July, 1819. Suspensions $112.91.
Ferris, William B. ensign 30th	585.00	Advanced on account of bounties and contingencies.
Falionar, Jonathan H. lieutenant 14th	230.45	Balance on settlement, 17th October, 1818. Suspensions $26.50.
Fisher, Otis	840.50	No account rendered.
Fotterall, Stephen E. colonel 32d	1,301.00	No account rendered.
Ford, Stephen, lieutenant 8th	47.00	Balance on settlement, 11th December, 1819. Suspensions exceed the balance.
Ferguson, David B. paymaster Maryland militia	472.31	Balance on settlement, 24th January, 1820. Suspensions for want of proper vouchers $250.38.
Foster, John, captain 22d infantry	1,054.21	Do do 12th February, 1819. Suspensions $689.25. Reported for suit 27th Sept. 1820.
Fay, Heman, A. Albany, New York	.17	Do do 1st June, 1815.
Forward, Daniel, lieutenant 25th	803.00	Advanced on account of bounties, &c.
Fisher, Meredith W. lieutenant 17th	673.80	Balance on settlement, 10th July, 1819. Suspensions $342.
Felton, Skelton, lieutenant 9th	292.00	Accounts rendered, and apparent balance due $169.30. Says his vouchers have been lost.
Follett, Charles, late captain 11th	3,248.00	Balance on settlement, 8th November, 1819, and reported for suit 24th November, 1819.
Green, George H. paymaster	19.60	Do do 21st May, 1820. Suspensions $8.39.

STATEMENT--Continued

Names and Rank	Amount Dolls.Cts.	Remarks
Goodwin, Robert M. lieutenant 3d infantry	350.00	Advanced him on account of bounties, &c.
Gustino, Amos, lieutenant 4th rifle	42.02	Balance on settlement, 10th October, 1816.
Gookin, Nathaniel, lieutenant 34th	630.00	Accounts rendered, and apparent balance due $599.
Green, James, lieutenant 11th	863.00	Advanced on account of bounties, pay, and contingencies.
Goodrick, Valentine R. lieutenant 11th	55.00	Advanced on account of bounties, &c.
Gale, Wm. jr., cornet	2,884.00	Balance on settlement, 26th September, 1820, and reported for suit 17th October, 1820.
Garrard, William, jr. captain volunteer cavalry	150.00	Advanced on account of volunteers.
Galloway, Samuel, major volunteers,	120.00	Advanced on account of pay of the army.

STATEMENT--Continued

Names and Rank	Amount Dolls.Cts.	Remarks
Gardiner, Benjamin D. ensign	100.00	Balance on settlement, 2d April, 1814.
Gillis, James, cornet	53.33	Advanced on account of pay of the army.
Glynn, Anthony G. paymaster 10th	89,282.00	Accounts and vouchers rendered, and apparent balance $551.81. Under examination.
Gibson, John, acting governor In. territory	5,644.16	Balance on settlement, 14th February, 1814. $4,194.16 on account of militia, and $1,450 advanced on account of bills drawn for supplies of the militia in Indiana territory, and to a detachment Under the command of Colonel Russell.
Graham, Henry R. captain riflemen	20.00	On account of contingencies, it being an over payment on the settlement of his accounts, 17th of August, 1814. Ascertained on a revision of his accounts at the Treasury. Per Comptroller's letter, dated 13th of June, 1816.
Greenwell, Philip P. lieutenant 5th	278.00	Accounts and vouchers rendered. Apparent balance due $19.23.
Gobert, Charles, contractor	2,850.00	Advanced on account of ordnance. It being on account of his Contract for the manufacture of musket balls.
Graves, Thomas C. lieutenant 17th	200.00	Advanced on account of bounties and contingencies.
German, Walter, ensign 3d dragoons	31.40	Balance on settlement, 8th January, 1820.
Glenn, Henry, assistant deputy quartermaster	516.81	Balance on settlement, 15th June, 1814.
Gilbreath, John, ensign 24th infantry	507.68	Balance on settlement, 12th September, 1816.
Gilbert, John, ensign 30th	1,100.00	Advanced on account of bounties, &c.
Gridley, Giles, acting surgeon	5.46	Balance on settlement, 22d March, 1814.
Green, James, lieutenant colonel militia	1,250.00	Advanced on account of quartermaster department $250, and by colonel Woolsey, $1,000.
Gwinn, Daniel, lieutenant 24th	20.00	Balance on settlement, 20th January, 1820.
Goode, John, lieutenant 26th	450.00	Accounts rendered, and apparent balance due $276.
Gill, John, captain sea fencibles	19.81	Balance on settlement, 21st May, 1814.
Grimes, Asa, lieutenant 31st	135.00	Accounts rendered, and apparent balance due $79.90.
Gourdine, W. captain, 43d	10.00	Advanced on account of contingencies.
Goodwin, Robert H. ensign 10th	82.18	Advanced on account of contingencies.
Gaines, John, paymaster 9th Virginia militia	13,422.00	Accounts and vouchers rendered, and apparent balance $440.54. Under examination.
Gresham, Lemuel, lieutenant	734.05	Balance on settlement, 24th December, 1816. Suspensions $24.
Gray, Nathaniel, inspector general	97.50	Advanced on account of quartermaster department.
Gibson, George, major	93.00	Balance on settlement, 23d May, 1815.

STATEMENT--Continued

Names and Rank	Amount Dolls.Cts.	Remarks
Gibson, William, lieutenant 36th	200.00	Accounts rendered, and apparent balance due $52.54.
Getz, George, captain 4th rifle	565.44	Balance on settlement, 22d January, 1820. Suspensions $396.31.
Gassaway, John, lieutenant 7th	42.36	Advanced on account of contingencies, for the transportation of his baggage.
Gilmore, Robert, captain Ohio militia	43.00	Advanced him on account of quartermaster department.
Granger, Orin, lieutenant 19th	1,200.00	Advanced on account of bounties, &c.
Grantt, John S. lieutenant, 17th	307.19	Balance on settlement, 26th October, 1816. Suspensions are more than this balance.

STATEMENT--Continued

Names and Rank	Amount Dolls.Cts.	Remarks
Gilman, Harvey, ensign 31st	287.35	Balance on settlement, 2d July, 1816. Suspensions, $12.
Gray, James, lieutenant 39th	188.00	Advanced on account of bounties, &c. Since received a credit of $12.
Greer, Andrew, lieutenant	778.00	Balance on settlement, 18th January, 1820
Gray, James, lieutenant 17th	706.99	Do do 4th April, 1817, $622.99, and an advance of $84 on account of pay of the army, making a balance of $706.79.
Giles, E. M. lieutenant artillery	236.40	Balance on settlement, 20th July, 1818. $46.40 on account of quartermaster department, and $190 advanced him on account of bounties, pay, and contingencies.
Gleason, Joseph, captain 5th infantry	926.00	Balance on settlement, 20th October, 1819.
Graham, John A. lieutenant	300.00	Advanced on account of quartermaster department.
Griffith, Thomas, lieutenant 28th	2,217.42	Balance on settlement, 18th June 1818. Suspensions requiring proper vouchers, $856.75.
Gray, T. V. deputy quartermaster general	25,393.38	Amount of provisions receipted for to the contractor, the issue of which has not been satisfactorily established.
Gray, Thomas B. lieutenant 18th	4.00	Balance on settlement, 18th June, 1818. Suspension of $4.
Grantland, Samuel, lieutenant 12th	300.00	Do do 5th July, 1817; $125 on account of bounties, &c. and $175 advanced him on account of pay and contingencies.
Green, William G. captain 4th riflemen	1,294.17	Do do 10th March, 1820. Arising from suspensions.
Gardner, Benjamin A.D.Q.M.G.	6,177.86	Do do 12th August, 1817, $5,049.58, and an advance of $1,128.28 on account of quartermaster department. Has other claims.
Gibson, James, captain, 12th	182. 6	Do do 2d September, 1819
Gates, James, Ohio militia	100.00	Advanced to pay his company, Ohio militia.
Greenaugh, Parker, lieutenant, 4th	126. 6	Balance on settlement, 25th August, 1817. Suspensions $23.
Gookin, I. W. captain	2,125.00	Do do 18th January, 1819. Reported for suit, 27th September, 1820.
Goodall, John captain	1,522.94	Do do 1st June, 1818. Suspensions $524.75.
Garrett, Henry, captain 43d	371.16	Do do 2nd October, 1819. Suspensions $215. 1.
Gookin, Supply B. lieutenant, 34th	274.70	Do do 10th January, 1820. Suspensions $74.70.
Goodenow, Rufus K. captain, 33d	68.56	Do do 22d April, 1820. Suspensions $6.20.
Goode, Robert, lieutenant artillery	846.50	Do do 29th July, 1818. Suspensions $28.
Gregory, Nehemiah, major 27th	804.92	Do do 6th January, 1820. Suspensions $260.
George, Daniel, lieutenant 45th	39. 4	Do do 10th July, 1818. Suspensions $8.

STATEMENT--Continued

Names and Rank	Amount Dolls.Cts.	Remarks
Gansevoort, John, assistant deputy paymaster	4,464. 8	Do do 20th November, 1817. Reported for suit, 28th May, 1818.
Gates, John, paymaster artillery	62.00	Advanced on account of bounties, &c.
Guy, John R. lieutenant	133.76	Balance on settlement, 20th January, 1818. Has rendered accounts Without vouchers for $244.82
Grafton, Joseph, major 21st	608. 3	Do do 28th March, 1818. Suspensions for $192.18.
Gray, Robert, major	580.00	Advanced on account of pay, contingencies, and quartermaster department, $330. $250 since received of R. Dennis in addition.

Names and Rank	Amount Dolls.Cts.	Remarks
Gray, James S lieutenant riflemen	490.00	Accounts and vouchers rendered for $253.24. Written to on the subject.
Grover, John, late paymaster New York militia	484.67	Balance on settlement, 20th April, 1818.
Gardner, Robert S. lieutenant and paymaster 13th	3,581.42	Do do 21st April, 1820. Reported for suit, 3d October, 1820.
Goodwin, Jeremiah, lieutenant and paymaster 33d	114. 7	Do do August, 1820.
Gregg, Daniel, captain, 45th	8.00	Do do 3d June, 1818. Suspensions $8.
Gilmore, Andrew, ensign riflemen	303.13	Do do 5th January, 1819.
Garrard, John M. paymaster 4th Kentucky militia	712.71	Do do 3d December, 1819. Suspensions $313.93.
Grayham, Richard, major	60.14	Do do 1st July, 1818. Suspensions to this amount.
Greenup, Wilson P. 1st Kentucky volunteer militia	36,156.34	Written to on the subject of his account, 11th June, 1817. Reported for suit, 9th July, 1818.
Gibson, James, colonel 4th	12,461.63	Reported for suit, 22d July, 1818.
Griffin, James S. lieutenant 38th	383.13	Balance on settlement, 22d January, 1820. Suspensions $10. Reported for suit, 17th October, 1820.
Gordon, Smith W. lieutenant 44th	110.00	Do Do 12th August, 1818. Suspensions $110.
Geslin, Francis, hospital surgeon	30.00	Advanced on account of medical and hospital department.
Gill, William, captain 19th	262.75	Balance on settlement, 8th October, 1818. Reported for suit, 17th October, 1820.
Gwynne, David, paymaster Ohio militia	165.31	Do do 18th June, 1819.
Green, James, lieutenant 3d riflemen	806.49	Do do 3d November, 1818. Suspensions $245.14. Reported for suit, 17th October, 1820.
Griswold, Joseph, captain	40.00	Advanced on account of bounties, &c.
Green, James, captain, and assistant deputy quartermaster general	168.50	Balance on settlement, 6th September, 1819.
Gaines, Thompson, paymaster 7th Kentucky militia	184. 7	Do do 7th November, 1820.
Gates, Jonas, lieutenant 31st	120.22	Do do 16th January, 1819.
Gray, George, lieutenant riflemen	893.95	Do do 1st February, 1819. Reported for suit 27th September, 1820. Suspensions $62.
Gholson, James, Kentucky militia	19,737.90	Accounts on file, and under examination.
Geyer, Henry S. paymaster 38th	4,761.93	Balance on settlement, 11th January, 1820. Suspensions $258.49. Reported for suit, 1st June, 1819.
Gibson, Robert, lieutenant 34th	90.59	Do do 28th June, 1819. Suspensions $29.
Gleim, Christian, paymaster Pennsylvania militia	1,017.22	Do do 29th May, 1820. In suit.
Goodwyn, Burwell, lieutenant, 10th	192.63	Do do 28th May, 1829. Suspensions $31.

STATEMENT--Continued

Names and Rank	Amount Dolls.Cts.	Remarks
Gibbs, Abel, lieutenant 30th	224.00	Advanced on account of bounties, &c.
Gates, A. ensign	1,000.00	Advanced on account of bounties, &c.
Garrett, Ashton, paymaster 17th	39,703.56	Balance on settlement, 19th August, 1819. Suspensions $30.38. Reported for suit, 5th November, 1819.
Greenwood, Miles, captain, 16th	298.00	Do. do. 20th July, 1820.

Names and Rank	Amount Dolls.Cts.	Remarks
Gutridge, William, ensign, 26th	112.00	Advanced on account of bounties, &c.
Goodwin, Kenmel, lieutenant 14th	100.00	Advanced on account of pay of the army, and quartermaster department.
Goddard, Lewis, lieutenant New York volunteers	185.00	Advanced on account of pay of the army.
Graves, Abraham, ensign New York militia	50.00	Advanced on account of pay of the army.
Gardiner, Charles K. major 25th	1,407.00	Advanced on account of bounties, &c. $57.50 of which being on account of transportation of baggage. He has accounts to render.
Griswold, William, paymaster New York militia	226.72	Balance on settlement, 8th June, 1820. Has additional claims.
Gordon, Willie J. lieutenant 10th	2,222.00	Do. do. 9th November, 1819. Suspensions $344. Reported for suit, 24th November, 1819.
Gantt, John, New York militia	31,695.02	Accounts on file and under examination.
Gillespie, George paymaster New York militia	1,362.99	Balance on settlement, 26th December, 1819. Suspensions, $1039.40
Gano, John S. Ohio militia	758.58	Accounts on file and under examination.
Hunter, David, lieutenant 12th	143.65	Balance on settlement, 15th March, 1814.
Henshaw, William S.	274.06	Do. do. 1st June, 1816.
Hairston, Samuel, lieutenant 20th	76.21	Do. do. 11th February, 1820.
Howard, Joshua, lieutenant 9th	50.00	Advanced on account of bounties, &c.
Haile, William F. ensign 11th	410.00	Advanced on account of bounties, pay, and contingencies.
Hazard, W. W. hospital surgeon's mate	700.00	Advanced on account of medical and hospital department.
Hite, R. G. Assistant adjutant general	270.00	Balance on settlement, 11th November, 1816, $120. He has received an additional sum of $150, making a balance of $270 against him.
Hull, Abraham F. captain 9th	859.81	Accounts rendered, and apparent balance due $576.41.
Hammons, Moses, ensign 33d	10.00	Balance on settlement, 24th January, 1820. Suspensions to this amount.
Hoxey, Thomas, Georgia militia	64,700.00	Accounts rendered, and apparent balance refunded.
Hurce, John, captain militia	120.00	Advanced on account of pay of the army.
Hazard, William, lieutenant	11.06	Balance on settlement, 27th August, 1816. Suspensions $51.
Hanham, Jams R. captain artillery	1,810.33	Advanced on account of bounties, quartermaster department, camp equipage, &c.
Hunt, Jedh. Captain militia	120.00	Advanced on account of pay of the army.
Hill, Henry O. lieutenant 5th infantry	301.40	Advanced on account of pay, subsistence, and bounties, &c.
Hawkins, Thomas, ensign 17th	100.00	Advanced on account of bounties and contingencies.
Holt, David, captain 17th	2,710.00	Advanced on account of bounties, pay, and contingencies.

STATEMENT--Continued

Names and Rank	Amount Dolls.Cts.	Remarks
Harris, Thomas, lieutenant 20th	440.32	Advanced on account of bounties, pay, and contingencies.
Hovey, George W. lieutenant 4th	33.96	Advanced on account of contingencies; being for transportation of his baggage.
Hays, Walter G. lieutenant 20th	2,354.55	Balance on settlement, 27th January 1820. Suspensions requiring additional vouchers, $30. Reported for suit, 27th September, 1820.
Hawkins, Philemon, captain 2d	13.13	Balance on settlement, 23d November, 1816. Suspensions, $179.
Harrison, Thomas, lieutenant 21st	100.00	Advanced on account of contingencies.

Names and Rank	Amount Dolls.Cts.	Remarks
Helm, H. P. lieutenant 7th	430.00	Advanced on account of bounties and contingencies.
Huber, Henry, lieutenant 38th	20.00	Advanced on account of contingencies.
Harrison, Richard M. lieutenant 23d	112.76	Balance on settlement, 7th February, 1814.
Harney, J. B. surgeon 3d infantry	22.58	Advanced on account of quartermaster department.
Hughes B. assistant deputy quartermaster general	149.89	Balance on settlement, 19th May, 1815, $694.25, to which add 1 dollar subsequently to his debt. He has refunded $545.36, leaving a balance of $149.89.
Howell, Lewis, lieutenant 19th	220.51	Balance on settlement, 7th March, 1814.
Hall, A. major general militia	982.74	Advanced on account of quartermaster department and contingencies.
Hobart, H. H. lieutenant artillery	245.00	Balance on settlement, 33d March, 1820.
Hall, John, captain	1,650.00	Do. do. 16th September, 1816. Suspensions $42. States to have lost $1,670, by unavoidable accident.
Hines, Abner, lieutenant 24th	20.00	Advanced on account of pay of the army.
Holmes, Bartlett, master mason	50.00	Advanced on account of quartermaster department.
Hinkley, Nathaniel, ensign 21st	304.61	Balance on settlement, 19th November, 1816, $254.61, and an advance of $50. on account of quartermaster department, making the balance of $304.61. Suspensions $297.74.
Howard, Lewis, captain,	100.00	Advanced on account of bounties, &c.
Hargis, Thomas F. lieutenant 32d	783.33	Advanced on account of bounties and contingencies.
Hall, George K. lieutenant 32d	133.33	Advanced on account of bounties and contingencies.
Hamilton, Joshua, captain riflemen	666.00	Balance on settlement, 21st February, 1816, $466, and an advance of $200 made him subsequently, making a balance of $666, due by him.
Herriott, Thomas, lieutenant dragoons	806.00	Balance on settlement, 18th March, 1820. Suspensions requiring further vouchers, amounting to $152.50.
Hogan, John, captain 39th	70.00	Advanced him on account of contingencies.
Hawkins, Perry, lieutenant	22.25	Advanced on account of contingencies.
Harrey, Benjamin, lieutenant 3d	350.00	Advanced on account of bounties, pay, and contingencies.
Hightower, Richard, captain 17th	1,200.00	Advanced on account of bounties and contingencies.
Hayes, A. H. lieutenant dragoons	741.92	Accounts rendered; he is chargeable with other moneys in addition to those here charged against him, exhibiting a balance of $807.92.
Hunter, George H. major	370.00	Advanced on account of bounties, &c.
Hood, John, lieutenant	50.00	Advanced on account of contingencies.
Hutchinson, Joseph, lieutenant 25th	208.45	Balance on settlement, 23d July, 1816. Suspensions $75.25.

STATEMENT--Continued

Names and Rank	Amount Dolls.Cts.	Remarks
Helms, F. T. lieutenant 13th	58.00	Advanced on account of quartermaster department.
Hardaway, Benjamin, ensign	700.23	Balance on settlement, 12th July, 1816.
Holmes, A. H. captain 8th	534.00	Accounts rendered.
Heath, L. lieutenant	200.00	Advanced on account of quartermaster department.
Henderson, Richard H. quartermaster militia	1,000.00	Advanced on account of quartermaster department.

STATEMENT--Continued

Names and Rank	Amount Dolls.Cts.	Remarks
Hopewell, John, lieutenant 12th	685.00	Balance on settlement 9th March, 1816.
Heet, Jacob, ensign 6th	60.00	Advanced on account of contingencies.
Halloway, Edward, lieutenant	110.63	Balance on settlement 14th October, 1816.
Heard, B.J. lieutenant	29.93	Ditto ditto 27th June, 1816.
Hall, Mortimer D. captain	1,300.00	Accounts and vouchers rendered for $1055.96, leaving an apparent balance due $244.04
Huntington, H. W. lieutenant 37th	4.00	Balance on settlement, 27th June, 1816.
Hopkins, T. S. brigadier general militia	50.00	Advanced on account of quartermaster department.
Hull, William, captain volunteers	400.00	Advanced on account of contingencies.
Hawley, Gideon, lieutenant, 27th	40.01	Balance on settlement 30th April, 1816.
Harper, Samuel	50.00	Advanced on account of bounties, &c.
Hahn, Michael, lieutenant 27th	200.00	Advanced on account of bounties, &c.
Hughes, William, lieutenant 17th	180.00	Accounts rendered, and apparent balance due $158.
Hacket, John S. lieutenant 24th infantry	170.00	Advanced on account of bounties, &c.
Humphreys, Carlisle, surgeon's mate	20.00	Advanced on account of contingencies.
Hyde, Thomas, captain, 43d	248.95	Balance on settlement, 29th December, 1818. Suspensions for proper vouchers, $188.17.
Houston, Mosman, major	3,303.00	Do. do. 14th October, 1816. Suspensions $790.88, and reported for suit, 27th September, 1819.
Harbaugh and Potter, contractors	7.38	Do. do. 7th April, 1817.
Hoyt, Paul G. late ensign 11th	32.36	Do. do. do. do. Suspensions $66.
Hindman, Thomas C lieutenant 39th	516.44	Do. do. 10th do. do. $24.
Hall, Henry, captain of dragoons	1,207.65	Do. do. 26th June, 1820. Claims additional credits.
Hopkins, Samuel G. captain cavalry	25,888.98	Do. do. 3d September, 1819. Reported for suit, 14th September, 1819.
Harrison, Thomas J. in service	4,364.00	Accounts rendered without vouchers for $174. Apparent balance of $4190. He sates he will render his accounts as soon as Possible.
Hathaway, Simon, ensign 30th	566.52	Balance on settlement, 9th November, 1818. Suspensions $512.
Hyde, Russel B. lieutenant	56.20	Do. do. 20th September, 1817.
Howard, George, captain 25th	734.64	Do. do. 6th March, 1817. Has further claims which he has promised to furnish the vouchers for.
Hampton, Wade, major general	5,623.00	Do. do. 9th May, 1817. $4623. Since received from Israel Smith, $1000.

STATEMENT--Continued

Names and Rank	Amount Dolls.Cts.	Remarks
Hopkins, Charles B. lieutenant, &c.	1,086.19	Do. do. 28th September, 1818. Reported for suit, 20th October, 1819.
Halse, James P. ensign 2d riflemen	156.80	Do. do. 27th June, 1817. Suspensions $170.
Harrison, Charles L. lieutenant 2d	976.71	Do. do. 10th November, 1819.
Hedelson, John, lieutenant 3d	510.00	Advanced on account of bounties, &c.
Hall, Edmund, ensign, 28th	280.00	Advanced on account of bounties and contingencies.
Hamilton, George, lieutenant 41st	36.00	Balance on settlement, 28th May, 1817, arising from suspensions.
Helm, Lina T. lieutenant 1st infantry	240. 89	Do. do. 1st June, 1817, $160.89. Suspensions $24. The sum of $80 since advanced on account of quartermaster department.

Names and Rank	Amount Dolls.Cts.	Remarks
Hight, George, lieutenant artillery	3,706.85	Balance on settlement, 1st June, 1817. Suspensions, $1050.30. Reported for suit, 5th November, 1819.
Henderson, Daniel, lieutenant 21st	2,839.60	Do. do. 16th June, 1817. Suspensions $213.49. Reported for suit 9th November, 1820.
Harris, James, lieutenant 40th	10.60	Do. do. 26th June, 1817. Suspensions $11.
Humphreys, Charles, captain 41st	871.14	Do do. 30th June, 1817. Suspensions $703.56. $167.58 since brought to his debit.
Holden, Daniel, captain 45th	16.00	Do. do. 17th August, 1817.
Hall, Elisha T. paymaster 7th infantry	91,468.71	Sundry vouchers rendered, and claims a balance of $627.39.
Hall, E. T. lieutenant 7th infantry	301.38	Balance on settlement, 5th July, 1817, $101.38; and he is subsequently charged with $200 for pay of the army.
Hicks, Abner H. lieutenant 35th	40.00	Do. do. 12 July, 1817.
Hoffman, Fred. W. lieutenant, 28th	30.00	Do. do. Advanced on account of contingencies.
Harges, Thomas F lieutenant 32d	751.15	Balance on settlement, 13th July, 1818. Suspensions $89.40
Henderson, Joseph, lieutenant 22d	1,454.70	Do. do. 20th November, 1819. Suspensions $854.69.
Hall, Robert R. lieutenant 22d	246.71	Do. do. 20th May, 1817.
Horrell, Thomas, lieutenant 16th	893.79	Do. do. 20th July, 1820, $393.70. He is subsequently charged with $500.
Hall, Elisha, captain, 45th	183.86	Do. do. 21st August, 1817. Suspensions, $14.
Hughes, Matthew, lieutenant 12th	735.00	Do. do. 21st March, 1820.
Hayes, Hanson, lieutenant 23d	53.50	Do. do. 15th September, 1820. Suspensions $252.
Harmond, Silas, paymaster N. Y. militia	26.97	Do. do. 17th August, 1820. Suspensions $9.86.
Hawkins, Abraham, captain, 4th	63.95	Do. do. 3d September, 1817. Suspensions $49.36.
Hatch, John, lieutenant 31st	428.10	Do. do. 2d September, 1817, $78.10. Suspensions $78, and he has subsequently been charged with the sum of $350, making a balance against him of $428.10.
Hugunin, Daniel, lieutenant 13th	953.05	Balance on settlement, 1st October, 1817.
Hopkins, Joseph, lieutenant 11th	684.51	Do. do. 3d October, 1817.
Haynie, Elijah, lieutenant 24th	296.60	Do. do. 28th August, 1818. Suspensions $86.
Holden, Caleb H. lieutenant 17th	1,987.09	Do. do. 2d January, 1818. Suspensions $754.08
Hickcox, Samuel B. lieutenant 29th	448.00	Do. do 22d December, 1817.
Hogeboom, Peter L. paymaster 23d	15,669.41	Do. do. 15th May, 1820. Suspensions $3,992.14, and Reported for suit, 3d October, 1820.
Henry, Spottswood, captain 2d	656.61	Do. do. 21st March, 1814, $456.61; and he has subsequently been charged with $200, making this balance.

STATEMENT--Continued

Names and Rank	Amount Dolls.Cts.	Remarks
Hill, Samuel R. ensign 23d	346.25	Balance on settlement, 28th May, 1819, $326.25. Suspensions of $28.20; and he has been charged with $200 making this balance.
Harper, James W. captain 27th	519.13	Balance on settlement, 18th February, 1818. Suspensions $590.50.
Hollingshead, John, lieutenant dragoons	241.35	Do. do. do.
Hendrix, Henry, ensign, 30th	426.94	Do. do. 21st August, 1818.
Hobart, William F. lieutenant artillery	5,459.00	Accounts rendered, without vouchers, for $2,517.75. Apparent balance $2,907.25. Written to on the subject 22d January, 1820.

STATEMENT--Continued

Names and Rank	Amount Dolls.Cts.	Remarks
Haring, Samuel, captain 13th	6,526.29	Balance on settlement, 16th May, 1818, $6471.29. Suspensions $16. Reported for suit, 17th September, 1819. $50 since received of John Chrystie.
Holmes, David, governor	648.62	Balance on settlement, 9th April, 1816.
Huntington, Samuel, late paymaster	38,776.52	Accounts and vouchers rendered. Apparent balance $462.93.
Hayne, Arthur P. inspector general	200.00	Accounts rendered, and apparent balance $130.
Hamilton, John, lieutenant 17th	102.66	Balance on settlement, 3d April, 1820
Hickham, H. H. captain 17th	1,799.82	Accounts rendered, and apparent balance due $1,655.82.
Harrison, Batteal, captain, 2d rifle	2,038.00	Balance on settlement, 8th June, 1816, $1,758. He is also charged with $280, making a balance against him of $2,038.
Hart, Richard G. paymaster 4th Kentucky militia	859.27	Balance on settlement, 22d June, 1819. Suspensions, $856.53.
Hopkins, David T. lieutenant 21st	300.00	Advanced on account of bounties, &c.
Hamilton, Alexander, captain 41st	227.37	Balance on settlement, 28th June, 1818. Arising from suspensions.
Hoppock, John L. captain	600.00	Advanced on account of bounties, &c.
Harrison, George, paymaster 8th infantry,	20,248.00	Reported for suit, 9th July, 1818.
Hallum, George, captain 39th	112.50	Balance on settlement, 24th March, 1819. Suspensions $62.50.
Henry, William Captain 3d artillery	20.00	Advanced on account of quartermaster department.
Henry, William mounted gun men	18,646.63	Accounts on file, and under examination.
Hewson, Thomas, wagon master	300.00	Advanced on account of quartermaster department.
Hathaway, Joshua, quartermaster N. Y. militia	100.00	Advanced on account of quartermaster department.
Hedges, Frederick E. lieutenant 5th	187.25	Balance on settlement, 11th July, 1818. Suspensions $92.
Herrin, David, lieutenant 26th	13.39	Do do 16th February, 1820.
Hukill, Levi, lieutenant 1st dragoons	294.63	Do do 18th July, 1818. Suspensions $175.
Hoyt, John, deputy wagon master	60.00	Advanced on account of quartermaster department.
Hall, Elijah, captain volunteers	55.93	Advanced on account of quartermaster department.
Hackley, James, lieutenant 17th	3,550.00	Balance on settlement, 29th October, 1819; and reported for suit, 10th November, 1819.
Hartell, Christian, captain, 27th	68.00	Do do 17th November, 1819.
Herron, James, captain, 29th	417.97	Do do 16th May, 1820.
Harris, John, lieutenant 6th infantry	857.45	Balance on settlement, 8th October, 1818. Suspensions made thereon, For want of proper vouchers, $713.46, and reported for suit, 27th September, 1820.
Herbert, Hardy, paymaster 2d Georgia militia	30,862.00	Accounts and vouchers rendered.
Hazleton, John, lieutenant 19th	676.29	Balance on settlement, 23d October, 1818.
Hockaday, John, Kentucky militia	16,437.63	Accounts on file, and under examination.

STATEMENT--Continued

Names and Rank	Amount Dolls.Cts.	Remarks
Hays, Michael C captain 1st riflemen	299.16	Balance on settlement, 2d November, 1818. Suspensions, 12 dollars.
Hedges, James, captain, 26th	1,366.32	Do do 14th do do and reported for suit, 27th September, 1819.
Harrison, Russell, lieutenant 12th	1,945.33	Do do 12th do 1819. Suspensions, $259.06, and reported for suit, 24th Nov. 1819.

STATEMENT--Continued

Names and Rank	Amount Dolls.Cts.	Remarks
Hindman, Jacob, lieutenant colonel	292.63	Balance on settlement, 5th May, 1820
Hammond, Lloyd T. late paymaster, 32d Md. Militia	900.70	Do do 23d February, 1819. Suspensions, $884.84.
Hutching, Charles, lieutenant 35th	98.30	Do do 14th April, 1819. Suspensions, $7.85.
Hall N. N. lieutenant	250.00	Advanced on account of bounties and contingencies.
Hunt, Jesse D. paymaster	31,527.00	Balance on settlement, 20th June, 1820. Suspensions, $7,060.75, and reported for suit, 25th Oct. 1820.
Harrison, William H. late governor	435.00	Advanced on account of quartermaster department.
Hall, John, lieutenant 19th	510.48	Balance on settlement, 2d March, 1819.
Heaton, William S. lieutenant, 11th	18.24	Do do 12th do
Hanson, Tunis, lieutenant 29th	35.64	Do do 7th December, 1819.
Hodges, Benjamin, paymaster 1st Maryland artillery	85.76	Do do 6th May, 1820.
Humphreys, Gad, captain 6th	12.00	Advanced on account of bounties, &c.
Hart, Henry, ensign	153.00	Balance on settlement, 22d August, 1820.
Huston, Wm. lieutenant 26th	238.00	Do do 9th April, 1819.
Hobbs, William C. lieutenant	100.00	Advanced on account of bounties, &c.
Henderson, John, lieutenant	50.00	Advanced on account of bounties, &c.
Henderson, John, paymaster Virginia Militia	809.78	Balance on settlement, 20th May, 1819. Suspensions $279.66. Reported, 28th October, 1820.
Holley, Samuel H. captain 11th	99.42	Do do 23d June, 1819.
Henton, Spencer, lieutenant 10th	480.00	Advanced on account of bounties, contingencies, and pay of the Army.
Huyck, John V. H. major	3,730.00	Balance on settlement, 12th November, 1819, and reported for suit, 24th November, 1819.
Homer, William S. hospital surgeon's mate	20.00	Advanced on account of contingencies.
Hughes, Matthew	735.00	Balance on settlement, 21st March, 1820. Suspensions, requiring additional vouchers, $60.
Hitchcock, Henry, Alabama militia	20,000.00	Accounts and vouchers rendered, and under examination.
Hayes, Joseph M to pay Ohio militia	314.94	Balance on settlement, 6th September, 1819.
Herrick, Oliver, captain volunteers	58.00	Advanced on account of pay of the army.
Hart, John D. lieutenant dragoons	675.57	Balance on settlement, 11th March, 1820. Suspensions, $642.23.
Head, Benjamin P. lieutenant 38th	606.00	Do do 5th October, 1819.
Hill, Josiah, lieutenant riflemen	30.00	Do do 22d do do.
Helms, Thomas A. captain dragoons	1,289.58	Do do 29th do do. $1,313.58. He has since received credit for $24, and reported for suit, 10th November, 1819.
Hunn, Peter F. New York militia	27,706.46	Accounts on file, and under examination.

STATEMENT--Continued

Names and Rank	Amount Dolls.Cts.	Remarks
Jett, William S. captain 20th	606.26	Balance on settlement, 16th September, 1816, $731.26, and he has subsequently received a credit for $125, leaving a balance against him of $606.26. Suspensions, $55.01.
Jackson, John, lieutenant 12th	1,600.00	Accounts rendered, and apparent balance, $1078.
Jacobs, Joseph K. ensign 9th	50.00	Advanced on account of bounties, &c.
Jewett, Ezekiel, ensign 11th	396.00	Balance on settlement, 16th December, 1816.

STATEMENT--Continued

Names and Rank	Amount Dolls.Cts.	Remarks
Johnson, Thomas, jun. Lieutenant, 24th	200.76	Accounts rendered; apparent balance due thereon $64.48.
Jenkins, M. lieutenant 3d artillery	1,080.00	Advanced on account of bounties, pay, and contingencies.
Johnson, Peter C. lieutenant 12th	927.33	Balance on settlement, 21st August, 1816. Suspensions, $530.59
Johnson, Lewis, quartermaster 26th	487.00	Advanced on account of contingencies and quartermaster department.
Johnson, Thomas S. lieutenant 2d infantry	220.00	Balance on settlement, 17th June, 1814; further accounts rendered, and not yet examined.
Johnson, John, captain 5th	208.88	Do do 14th July, 1820. Has additional vouchers.
Johnson, James, lieutenant 12th	175.50	Advanced on account of bounties, &c.
Jordon, Jonas, lieutenant 28th	100.00	Advanced on account of bounties, &c.
Jenkins, Joseph, lieutenant, 18th	1,500.00	Advanced on account of bounties and contingencies, &c.
Jenkins, John, captain 42d	2,356.00	Balance on settlement, 17th September, 1820, and reported for suit, 30th September, 1820.
Johnson, David	1,000.00	Advanced on account of quartermaster department.
Jones, Charles G. captain, 29th	300.00	Advanced on account of quartermaster department.
Johnson, Cyrus, captain 31st infantry	113.27	Balance on settlement, 15th August, 1814.
Jones, Henry B. lieutenant sea fencibles	113.00	Accounts rendered, upon which he claims a balance.
Jackman, Benjamin, lieutenant 21st	650.00	Advanced on account of bounties and contingencies.
Jones, Benjamin B. captain, 35th	602.03	Balance on settlement, 19th June, 1816, $642.03 He has since received a credit for 40 dollars.
Jorden, William, assistant deputy quartermaster general	1,000.00	Advanced on account of quartermaster department.
Jones, James I. New York militia	878.76	Balance on settlement, 30th October, 1820. Suspensions to nearly this amount.
Irwin, James	50.00	Advanced on account of quartermaster department.
Jerrison, John assistant deputy quartermaster general	42,666.76	On account of subsistence, being the amount of provisions received from Farish Carter, in 1815 at Fort Mitchell. Vouchers rendered not yet examined.
Johnson, S. lieutenant 13th	20.00	Advanced on account of contingencies.
Jesup, Thomas S. major	920.38	Balance on settlement, 9th May, 1817.
Johnson, Benjamin, captain riflemen	549.38	Do do 13th May, 1819.
Jones, William captain, 8th	475.32	Do do 24th June, 1817. Suspensions, $375.16.
Irby, Joseph, lieutenant 43d	79.40	Do do 8th May, 1818, $64.40. Suspensions $13. He is subsequently charged with $16.

STATEMENT--Continued

Names and Rank	Amount Dolls.Cts.	Remarks
Jennings, Robert C. D. commissary	190,334.71	Do do 18th August, $139,334.71. He is subsequently charged with $51,000, and reported for Suit, 14th September, 1819.
Irvine, Armstrong, captain 42d	1,130.20	Balance on settlement 3d October, 1817, $769.42. Suspensions $178; and he has since been charged with $360.78, making this balance.
Ingersol, Jared, lieutenant 9th	60,209.50	Advanced him on account of bounties, contingencies, pay, subsistence, and fortifications. Has rendered accounts in part.
Izard, George, major general	1,000.00	Advanced on account of pay of the army.
Jones, Terah, lieutenant and paymaster 16th	1,193.23	Balance on settlement, 26th November, 1819. Suspensions, $86.26. His accounts rendered, and under examination.

STATEMENT--Continued

Names and Rank	Amount Dolls.Cts.	Remarks
Jones, John, ensign 23d	300.00	Advanced on account of bounties and contingencies.
Jamison, John, Indian agent	100.00	Advanced on account of pay of the army.
Jewett, Matthew H. paymaster 28th	19,884.73	Balance on settlement, 25th May, 1818. Vouchers lost. An act has passed for his relief. Not settled for want of explanations relative to his charges, which are expected to be made.
Jackson, William B. lieutenant 1st infantry	602.00	Balance on settlement, 1st July, 1818. Suspensions, 16 dollars.
Johnson, William cornet	126.64	Advanced on account of pay and contingencies.
Jenkins, William, brig. Quartermaster New York militia	59.72	Advanced on account of quartermaster department.
Johnston, Littleton, ensign 24th	1,440.56	Balance on settlement, 10th July, 1818; and reported for suit, 27th September, 1819.
Jackson, George W. captain 17th infantry	228.75	Balance on settlement, 14th August, 1818, $71.75. Suspensions $10. He is subsequently charged with $157.
Jackson, George W. paymaster 19th infantry	16,425.25	Has lost his accounts and vouchers. Legislative interference is necessary.
Jones, Elisha, captain 9th	626.37	Balance on settlement, 17th September, 1818. Suspensions, $333.30.
Jaquett, Isaac, lieutenant 4th riflemen	225.29	Do do 19th do Suspensions $79.60.
Johns, Abijah, ensign 19th	207.69	Do do 1st October, 1818, $157.69. Suspensions, 66 dollars, and he has been subsequently charged with 50 dollars.
Johnston, George, lieutenant dragoons	30.00	Advanced on account of quartermaster department.
Johnston, William, lieutenant 24th	489.26	Balance on settlement, 11th November, 1818.
Jameson, James, militia	2,100.00	Accounts on file, and under examination.
Jones, William B. lieutenant 24th	16.00	Balance on settlement, 7th January, 1819.
Jones, Winfield, lieutenant 35th	669.30	Advanced on account of bounties, &c.
Jones, Edward, lieutenant 39th	133.62	Accounts rendered, and apparent balance, $117.84.
I'on, Jacob B. captain artillery	18.82	Balance on settlement, 21st February, 1819. Suspensions $36.82.
Johnson, James, to pay Kentucky volunteers	3,300.00	Accounts and vouchers rendered, upon which he claims a balance.
Johnson, Andrew, to pay Virginia militia	251.67	Advanced on account of pay and subsistence.
Jordon, A. S. to pay Pennsylvania militia	3,347.33	Advanced on account of pay, subsistence, and forage.
Jameson, James to pay Pennsylvania militia	1,200.00	Advanced on account of pay of the army.
Irvine, William, 10th infantry	142.00	Advanced on account of bounties, &c.
Johnson, Hezekiah, assist. dep. quartermaster general	382.38	Written to, on the 16th November, 1819, requiring his early attention to the liquidation of this account.
Keyes, Isaac, ensign, 12th	176.87	Balance on settlement, 24th May, 1814, $276.87. He has since refunded 100 dollars.

STATEMENT--Continued

Names and Rank	Amount Dolls.Cts.	Remarks
Kehz, John D. ensign	374.00	Do do 29th December, 1813, 204 dollars. He ha since been charged with 170 dollars.
Kay, Aaron, wagon master	200.00	Advanced on account of quartermaster department.
Kenan, Michael I. captain 10th	359.49	Balance on settlement, 16th May, 1820.
Knox, Ebenezer, ensign 21st	483.77	Do do 13th January, 1820. Suspensions, $201.33.
Kelly, Thomas D	130.00	Advanced on account of pay of the army.
Kent, Robert W. captain	23.72	Balance on settlement, 17th March, 1820. Suspensions, $23.62.
Kercheval, Samuel, lieutenant 7th	500.00	Advanced on account of bounties and contingencies.
Koontz, Jacob, lieutenant 20th	529.67	Balance on settlement, 25th February, 1817. Suspensions, $21.35.

STATEMENT--Continued

Names and Rank	Amount Dolls.Cts.	Remarks
Ketcham, Thomas, light artillery	254.34	Balance on settlement, 8th February, 1816.
Kelly, Hanson, deputy commissary	32,300.00	Accounts and vouchers rendered. Has refunded the sum of $1,703, the acknowledged balance.
Kerr, Archibald, lieutenant,	100.00	Advanced on account of contingencies.
Kean, Jesse, ensign 14th	264.48	Balance on settlement, 6th July 1815, $150.16. He has since received $114.32.
King, Charles, lieutenant 32d	1,409.52	Accounts rendered, and apparent balance due $692.84
King, Francis B. lieutenant 9th	400.00	Advanced on account of bounties and contingencies.
Kingsbury, Lawson, lieutenant 9th	75.00	Advanced on account of bounties, &c.
Kerrick, Oliver, captain	100.00	Advanced on account of pay of the army.
King, William, lieutenant 5th	200.00	Advanced on account of bounties, &c.
Kenney, Abraham contractor,	152.00	On account of subsistence, being the amount of provisions purchased by Robert Stewart, lieutenant 2d artillery, on the failure of of said Kenney to supply.
Kearney, Stephen W. captain 13th	478.00	Advanced on account of pay, bounties, and quartermaster department.
Ketcham, Gilbert, lieutenant colonel volunteers	2,432.07	Advanced by the paymaster general, on account of clothing.
Kirby, Samuel, lieutenant 35th	800.00	Advanced on account of bounties, &c.
Kendall, William, lieutenant	775.00	Advanced on account of bounties and contingencies.
Kerr, Daniel C. hospital surgeon	4,231.00	Advanced on account of quartermaster and hospital department.
Keenes, Melchor, lieutenant, 36th	200.00	Accounts rendered and apparent balance due $179.85.
Keys, Julius, brigade major	300.00	Advanced on account of contingencies.
Kenney, Joseph, captain, 25th	389.34	Balance on settlement, 14th April, 1817, $156. He is also charged with $233.34, on settlement, 27th May, 1814.
King, Philip, lieutenant 17th	500.00	Accounts rendered and apparent balance $156.38.
Keese, George, lieutenant 6th	565.07	Balance on settlement, 10th August, 1820.
Ketchum, David Major 25th	579.73	Do. do. 18th March, 1819. Suspensions $474.35.
Kennedy, John, captain, 2 riflemen	261.13	Do. do. 22d May, 1818. Suspensions, $84.48.
Keyser, George, major 38th	10,472.65	Do. do. 29th November, 1817, $10372.65. He is since charged with $100. Reported for suit, 24th December, 1817.
King, William, lieutenant artillery	1,039.97	Balance on settlement, 18th September, 1818. Suspensions $118.26.
Key, John, captain, 12th	2,128.48	Do do. 20th November, 1817.
Kavenaugh, Charles, major	6,069.63	Advanced on account of quartermaster department.
Kibbe, Noadiah, lieutenant 31st	491.94	Balance on settlement, 28th April, 1818. Suspensions $373.33.
Knapp, John, lieutenant, 15th infantry	1,968.00	Advanced on account of bounties, pay, contingencies and quartermaster department.

STATEMENT--Continued

Names and Rank	Amount Dolls.Cts.	Remarks
King, Thomas D. major 43d	851.88	Balance on settlement, 26th May, 1816. $881.38. Has since received credit for 30 dollars.
Keeth, Samuel, paymaster New York militia	433.38	Do. do. 1st September, 1820. Reported for suit, 17th June, 1818.
Kingsley, Ebenezer C. paymaster N.Y. volunteers	1,167.40	Do. do. 19th February, 1819. Suspensions $134.
Knapp, Philip, paymaster New York militia	67.74	Do do. 13th May, 1820. Reported for suit, 17th June, 1818.

STATEMENT--Continued

Names and Rank	Amount Dolls.Cts.	Remarks
Keller, William, lieutenant 3d riflemen	30.00	Advanced on account of contingencies.
Kinglsey, Alpha, deputy paymaster	1,101,876.51	Accounts and vouchers rendered, and apparent balance $48,804.96. Has further accounts to render, and vouchers to perfect, which he has been called upon for.
Kerr, Archibald, paymaster 5th cavalry, Md. Militia	1,407.52	Balance on settlement, 24th March, 1819. Suspensions, $1,178.71.
Kellog, Elisha, paymaster 4th New York militia	32.31	Do. do. 4th September, 1818.
Kelly, Daniel G. lieutenant 45th	50.84	Do. do. 15th September, 1818.
Kenney, Nicholas c. lieut. and quartermaster 12th	250.00	Accounts and vouchers rendered for $72. Apparent balance $178.
Keemle, Samuel, paymaster to Pennsylvania militia	153.40	Balance on settlement, 30th November, 1818. Suspensions $70.83.
Knight, Simeon, deputy paymaster	221,793.91	Accounts and vouchers rendered, and apparent balance $4,515.77.
Kincaid, John W. lieutenant	1,600.00	Account rendered, and claims credit for $71.25. Written to on the subject of his account, 10th Jan, 1820.
Knox, John, lieutenant 26th	197.24	Balance on settlement, 17th April, 1819, $253.24. Suspensions $178. He has since refunded $56.
Keiser, Christopher, lieutenant ordnance	363.75	Advanced on account of ordnance.
King, Edward, captain, 18th	1,776.81	Balance on settlement, 1st May, 1819. Suspensions $39.
Kinkead, Joseph, paymaster	598.66	Do. do. 12th June, 1820. Suspensions $18.91.
Kendrick, J. special commissary	93,980.25	Amount of provisions furnished by the contractor. Accounts have been received, but not satisfactory.
Kratzer, Samuel, to pay Ohio militia	3,555.43	Advanced on account of pay and subsistence.
King, Adam, act. P.M. to Battalion Columbia militia	223.85	Balance on settlement, 23d August, 1819.
Kenny, William, lieutenant artillery	.24	Do. do. 20th September, 1814, $183.50. He has since refunded to the P.M.G. $183.26.
Kerr, Joseph, under contract with Thomas Buford	3,434.05	Do. do. 11th September, 1819.
Kenney, John, lieutenant 12th	210.04	Do. do. 28th May, 1814, $140.04. Since been charged with $70.
Ketchlone, Charles, captain	280.00	Advanced on account of bounties, &c.
Kellogg, S. D. lieutenant 29th	1,910.06	Balance on settlement, 30th June, 1815, on account of bounties, &c. $810.06. He has since been charged with $1,100.
King, John, captain 23d	34.25	Advanced on account of bounties and contingencies.
Love, George, paymaster New York militia	610.68	Balance on settlement, 11th March, 1820. Suspensions $252.52.
Lawrence, Thomas, lieutenant 22d	362.05	do. do. 11th January, 1820
Lowe, Gideon, ensign	300.00	Advanced on account of bounties, &c.
Lee, Isaac, cornet militia	40.00	Advanced on account of militia.
Lyon, Thomas, captain 16th	228.00	Advanced on account of bounties, &c.

STATEMENT--Continued

Names and Rank	Amount Dolls.Cts.	Remarks
Lyon, Thomas, lieutenant, 16th	248.00	Balance on settlement, 26th July, 1820, and reported for suit 26th September, 1820.
Larned, Benjamin F.	1,020.91	
Leonard, Frederick, paymaster Delaware militia	342.92	Balance on settlement, 3d November, 1820. Has claims requiring additional vouchers to nearly this amount.
Leeth, James, lieutenant 39th	868.00	do. do. 14th January, 1820.
Luckett, I. R. N. lieutenant 2d infantry	240.00	Advanced on account of bounties &c.

STATEMENT--Continued

Names and Rank	Amount Dolls.Cts.	Remarks
Long, John B. captain, 39th	2,100.00	Accounts rendered and apparent balance due $1,590.
Libby, Daniel, captain, 21st	2,835.26	Accounts and vouchers rendered, apparent balance due $1,501.49. Additional accounts and vouchers received 13th November, 1820.
Leavitt, William, lieutenant 19th	1,260.00	Advanced on account of bounties, pay, and contingencies.
Lothorp, Charles, captain, 33d	157.41	Balance on settlement, 11th January, 1820
Lane, Daniel, lieutenant 33d	50.00	Advanced on account of bounties and contingencies.
Lomax, Edward L. lieutenant 5th	100.00	Advanced on account of camp equipage, &c.
Lithgow, William, lieutenant	30.00	do do
Leonard, Nathaniel, assistant deputy quartermaster	823.81	Balance on settlement, 28th November, 1816, $807.81; and an advance on account of bounties &c. of $16.
Law, Prentis, captain, 3d infantry	200.00	Advance him on account of bounties, &c.
Lythe, Robert, lieutenant sea fencibles	100.00	Advanced him on account of contingencies.
Luckett, Valentine P. ensign	724.00	Balance on settlement 16th February, 1820
Lee, Samuel M. paymaster dragoons	1,890.86	do do 18th September, 1820. Deceased. Sureties Written to same date on the subject of this balance.
Lewis, Henry, ensign 20th	80.00	Advanced on account of bounties, &c.
Lea, George W. ensign 38th	105.00	Balance on settlement, 17th February, 1820.
Leaken, S. C. captain 38th	50.00	Advanced on account of contingencies.
Lewis, Frederick, lieutenant and aid de camp	50.00	Advanced him to pay expenses of baggage wagon.
Loring, Joseph, colonel	28.00	Balance on settlement 15th September, 1816.
Larned, Charles, lieutenant 28th infantry	100.00	Advanced on account of bounties &c.
Lynch, John ensign 14th	102.91	Balance on settlement, 1st August, 1814.
Lane, Edmund, assistant deputy quartermaster general	121,366.80	This amount is for provisions receipted for by this officer. He has rendered evidences o the disposition of the greater part now under examination, and has made disposition to the actual delivery. Not yet settled.
Lovell, Joseph ensign 9th	20.00	Accounts and vouchers rendered for $10.39; apparent balance $9.61.
Lewis, William, lieutenant Kentucky militia	1,684.83	Advanced on account of pay, subsistence, and forage.
Lucas, John, captain 26th	700.00	accounts rendered; he has received additional sums of money brought to his debit, making an apparent balance of $1,130.
Lavall, William, lieutenant 3d infantry	970.00	Balance on settlement, 4th May, 1816.
Lockhart, Josiah, captain, 26th	42.68	Account rendered; he has received additional moneys to those here charged, leaving an apparent balance due $158.51.
Legon, William B. ensign 43d	55.51	Balance on settlement, 4th May, 1816.

STATEMENT--Continued

Names and Rank	Amount Dolls.Cts.	Remarks
Lynch, James, agent for Oneida iron manufact. compa.	1,007.27	Advanced on account of ordnance, for the supply of cannon balls.
Lucas, Edward, paymaster Virginia militia	24.79	Balance on settlement, 12th August, 1820.
Love, Granville N. ensign 17th	700.00	Advanced on account of bounties, &c.

STATEMENT--Continued

Names and Rank	Amount Dolls.Cts.	Remarks
Larwell, Joseph, lieutenant 2d infantry	60.00	Advanced on account of bounties, &c.
Lawson, John H. ensign 43d	350.00	Advanced on account of pay, bounties, & contingencies.
Lewis, James A. ensign 20th	348.00	Advanced on account of contingencies.
Lacey, John T.	500.00	Advanced on account of quartermaster department.
Loften, William M. lieutenant 3d rifle	2,228.78	Balance on settlement, 29th May, 1815.
Lewis, R., foragemaster Georgia militia	100.00	Advanced on account of quartermaster department.
Lane, M. M. lieutenant 33d	78.75	Balance on settlement, 23d July, 1816. Suspensions $76.
Lawrence, James, ensign 43d	220.00	Advanced on account of bounties and contingencies.
Lawson, John M. ensign	68.00	Accounts and vouchers rendered for $24. He has received additional monies making the balance against him $326.
Labugan, Bartholomew, assistant deputy paymaster	16,204.35	Balance on settlement, 23d August, 1819. Suspensions $213.52. Reported for suit, 1st June, 1819.
Lane, Isaac, colonel 33d	914.53	do do, 6th August, 1816, $602.88, and subsequently the sum of $231.65 has been charge against him, making the balance due by him $914.53
Lane, Daniel, major 33d	40.08	do do, 1st December, 1819.
Laval, Jacent, colonel dragoons	106.58	do do, 20th December, 1817.
Long, Nicholas, colonel 43d infantry	712.98	Balance on settlement, 23d December, 1816, $413.45, and $160.77 on settlement 17th June, 1817; and he is chargeable in addition, thereto with the sum of $127.75, making this balance against him.
Learned, Joseph D. colonel 34th	640.49	Advanced him on account of bounties, &c.
Lane, Rufus K. lieutenant 33d	102.16	Balance on settlement, 14th May, 1817. Suspensions $78.
Laprage, William, lieutenant 8th	218.44	do. do. 13th do. Suspensions $8.46.
Lewis, Cornelius N. lieutenant 2d riflemen	1,427.25	do. do. 7th June, 1819, and reported for suit 27th September, 1820.
Lequex, Peter, assistant deputy quartermaster general	26,576.08	Of this balance, $20,729.91 is for provisions receipted for to the contractor, vouchers for the issue of which are not regular; the balance is on his account as quartermaster, for which vouchers have been rendered in part. Suspended for explanation.
London, I. E. lieutenant 28th	1,300.00	Advanced on account of bounties, &c.
Ladd, Samuel, ensign 16th	520.58	Balance on settlement, 2d July, 1819.
Larkin, John, lieutenant 22d	1,694.68	do. do. 27th June, 1820.
Lee, Henry, major 36th	805.26	do. do. 26th August, 1817.

STATEMENT--Continued

Names and Rank	Amount Dolls.Cts.		Remarks
Lynds, Elam, captain, 29th	623.33 20.00	do.	do. 2d August, 1820. Claims additional credits nearly equal to the balance, the vouchers for which are wanting.
Lindsay, William, lieutenant colonel artillery		do.	do. 15th December, 1817.
Larrabe, Charles, major 3d infantry	1.00	do.	do. 25th February, 1820.
Lamb, Dudley, lieutenant 23d	293.00	do.	do. 22d June, 1819. Suspensions, $178.
Lee, Washington, deputy paymaster	9,950.00	do.	do. 25th April, 1818. This balance arose on settlement, in which he claimed a credit for $10,000 advanced, for which the voucher was not deemed sufficient. Suit was instituted for the balance, and judgment rendered for the defendant.

STATEMENT--Continued

Names and Rank	Amount Dolls.Cts.	Remarks
Levake, John, lieutenant 26th	839.85	Balance on settlement, 7th December, 1818. He has subsequently rendered vouchers for $7.50, and has an account for pay, &c. at the paymaster general's office. Suspensions $58.
Lewis, Aaron, lieutenant 9th	251.02	do. do. 24th July, 1818. Suspensions $244.25.
Lewis, William B.	12,297.69	do. do. 12th November, 1819. Has additional claims for compensation.
Lamar, Robert, lieutenant 8th	421.44	do. do. 15th May, 1818.
Lovett, Thomas C. ensign 8th	730.56	do. do. 10th April, 1819. Suspensions $62.
Langham, A. L.	2,572.00	Account rendered, on which he claims $430. Apparent balance $2142.
Lee, Charles W. lieutenant 15th	243.33	Balance on settlement, 10th September, 1818.
Lane, James, lieutenant	150.00	Advanced on account of bounties and contingencies.
Looker, Allison C. ensign riflemen	449.49	Balance on settlement, 22d April, 1819. Suspensions $32.
Lissenhoff, Frederick H. paymaster Georgia militia	7,398.60	Written to on the subject of his accounts, 25th February, 1818, and Reported for suit 17th June, 1818.
Lott, Abraham, New York militia	2,359.16	Balance on settlement, 10th November, 1820. Suspensions, $2298.
Lee, Richard H. paymaster	18,967.09	Reported for suit 20th May, 1820.
Leavenworth, Henry colonel	5,299.31	Balance on settlement, 19th June, 1818. Suspensions $15.
Lancaster, William, lieutenant 10th	970.12	do. do. 30th June, 1818. Suspensions $84.25
Lytle, John, captain	2,800.00	Advanced on account of quartermaster department.
Lyman, Chester, major	1,868.12	Balance on settlement, 26th September, 1818, $1,668.12. Suspensions $1424. He has since been charge with $200, making this balance.
Lewis, Morgan, general	225.00	Advanced on account of quartermaster department.\
Levake, Augustus, lieutenant 26th	25.00	Balance on settlement, 2d September, 1818.
Egate, Thomas C. lieutenant and quartermaster	157.31	do. do. 2d March, 1820
Langham, John S. paymaster Mich. Militia	4,797.10	do. do. 13th November, 1818. Suspensions $664.41.
Littlejohn, Leonard J. M. paymaster 3d Maryd. Mil.	609.75	do. do. 27th February, 1819.
Lyford, Fifield, lieutenant 31st	200.63	do. do. 26th March, 1819
Lee, Stephen, lieutenant 19th	1,001.67	do. do. 12th May, 1819. Suspensions, $912.77, and reported for suit, 27th September, 1820
Lane, Samuel, major 14th	912.52	do. do. 31st May, 1818. Suspensions, $50.
Livermore, Charles, lieutenant 13th	106.30	do. do. 24th June, 1819.
Legate, Samuel, lieutenant, 9th	2,031.93	do. do. 24th October, 1816, $1867.93. He has since charged with $164, making this balance.

STATEMENT--Continued

Names and Rank	Amount Dolls.Cts.	Remarks
Lane, Daniel C. quartermaster brig. Kentucky militia	935.00	do. do. 23d July, 1819.
Lee, John, lieutenant 34th	319.37	do. do. 29th July, 1819.
Leach, I. lieutenant 7th	200.00	Advanced on account of bounties &c.
Lomax, Mann P. major artillery	25.25	Balance on settlement, 12th May 1820.
Learned, Simon, colonel 9th	539.76	do. do. 14th October, 1815. $1298.88. Has since refunded to paymaster general $759.12, leaving him indebted this sum.

STATEMENT--Continued

Names and Rank	Amount Dolls.Cts.	Remarks
Lewis, Nicholas, issuing commissary, N. W. army	6,024.65	On account of subsistence, being the amount of provisions received from Joseph Kerr, at Upper Sandusky, for which he is held accountable until he shews the application thereof.
Langham, Elias T. captain 19th	100.00	Accounts and vouchers rendered, upon which he claims a balance.
Leake, Isaac Q. late paymaster	233.05	Balance on settlement, 10th November, 1819.
Long, Robert W. late ensign 14th	18.12	Advanced on account of contingencies.
Morrow, James, lieutenant 22d infantry	96.95	Balance on settlement, 21st February, 1817.
Morgan, Lewis, lieutenant 2d artillery	950.00	Accounts rendered, without vouchers for $717.12. Apparent Balance $212.88
Moore, Stephen H. captain volunteers	2,950.00	Advanced on account of volunteers and contingencies.
Morris, Robert H. captain	585.70	Balance on settlement, 30th June, 1813, $566; and, on settlement 20th August, 1816, $219.07; making this balance.
Meeker, James, lieutenant militia cavalry	150.00	Advanced on account of militia.
Marsteller, Ferdinand, captain militia, &c.	35,219.21	Balance on settlement, 27th December, 1815, $36,156.77. He has since been charged with $1,430.76, and, on settlement on his pay and subsistence account, 24th April, 1820, he has received a credit for $2,560.26, leaving this balance. He is dead, and insolvent.
McGuire, Samuel, captain 35th	1,674.00	Advanced on account of bounties and contingencies.
Morris, Horace, ensign 11th	48.00	Advanced on account of bounties, and pay of the army.
Morse, Samuel A. quartermaster	71.14	Advanced on account of contingencies.
Marlin, Ralph, major 22d	6,227.69	Advanced on account of bounties, pay, and contingencies.
Marcheval, Joseph, captain 14th	180.00	Balance on settlement, 12th September, 1820, and reported for suit 26th September, 1820.
Mitchell, Charles, lieutenant 19th	1,235.00	No accounts received.
Morril, Stephen, jr. ensign 34th	171.51	Account rendered without vouchers, upon which he claims a balance.
Moore, George	250.00	Advanced on account of quartermaster department.
McIntire, John B. ensign 34th	170.00	Advanced on account of bounties and contingencies.
Morse, Elias, ensign 34th	300.65	Accounts rendered for $210.40; vouchers only for $30, leaving an Apparent balance of $90.25.
Melier, William, governor North Carolina	440.04	Balance on settlement, 6th September, 1816.
Morrow, William, lieutenant 22d	200.00	Advanced on account of contingencies.
McIntire, John, lieutenant 3d rifle	8.29	Balance on settlement, 14th October, 1813. Suspensions $8.
Merrick, Joseph J. captain, 36th	2,350.00	Advanced on account of bounties and contingencies.

STATEMENT--Continued

Names and Rank	Amount Dolls.Cts.	Remarks
Messing, Frederick, ensign	65.00	Account rendered, and apparent balance $62.50.
Meeks, Alexander J. lieutenant 17th	192.00	Advanced on account of pay, bounties, and contingencies.
Murray, George, lieutenant 5th	50.00	Advanced on account of contingencies.
Morrison, Joseph, lieutenant 33d	834.75	Balance on settlement, 13th April, 1820; and reported for suit, 17th October, 1820.
Means, Thomas, captain 33d infantry	25.60	Balance on settlement, 26th July, 1814.
Malford, Clarence, agent	1,535.19	Advanced on account of completing fortifications, and pay of the army.
Marquand, Joseph, agent fortifications	500.00	Advanced on account of completing fortifications and barracks at Newburyport, Massachusetts.

STATEMENT--Continued

Names and Rank	Amount Dolls.Cts.	Remarks
Morse, Abel, lieutenant 6th	2.50	Balance on settlement, 9th February, 1820
Miller, John, deputy paymaster	19,401.09	Do do 15th March, 1814; stated that he had been robbed of the money. He petitioned Congress in the year 1813.
Morgan, Arthur, captain 7th	448.00	Advanced on account of bounties and contingencies.
Markle, Joseph, captain volunteers	1,200.00	Advanced on account of volunteers.
Macklay, Samuel, lieutenant artillery	200.00	Advanced on account of bounties, &c.
M'Kenzie, Charles C. lieutenant 3d rifle	78.79	Balance on settlement, 15th May, 1812.
Murray, Thomas, lieutenant artillery	244.00	Do do 12th March, 1812, $44. He has since been charged with $200, making this balance.
M'Kelvy, James S. captain	200.00	Advanced on account of bounties, &c.
Milton, Homer V. lieutenant colonel	1,997.62	Balance on settlement, 7th March, 1820, and reported for suit, 28th September, 1820.
Moore, Robert B. captain, 3d	447.33	Do do 31 January, 1817. Suspensions $61.50.
Mifflin, Benjamin, deputy commissary	459.43	Do 12th July 1813.
Morton, L. lieutenant 1st infantry	600.00	Advanced on account of bounties and contingencies.
Morgan, John E.	150.00	Advanced on account of contingencies.
M'Coll, John, surgeon's mate	55.00	Advanced on account of contingencies.
Morford, John, and James	350.00	Advanced them on account of ordnance.
M'Gee, James, lieutenant 22d	8.00	Advanced on account of quartermaster department.
M'Kenney, John T. lieutenant artillery	64.64	Advanced on account of contingencies, for his stage from Bent, Va. to Sackett's Harbor.
M'Whorter, John, captain 3d riflemen	2,225.20	Balance on settlement, 22d July, 1815, and reported for suit, 20th September, 1819. Has rendered vouchers for $580, and has a claim for arrears of pay, &c.
M'Clary, Andrew, captain 11th	34.00	Advanced him on account of bounties, &c.
Mason, T. lieutenant 36th	103.81	Balance on settlement, 27th April, 1815.
M'Crimmin, Daniel, adjutant 14th	250.00	Advanced on account of bounties and contingencies.
M'Donald, James, lieutenant 39th	154.01	Balance on settlement, 18th January, 1817. Suspensions $140.
Martin, Thomas J. lieutenant 16th	150.00	Advanced on account of bounties and contingencies.
M'Nair, D. D., lieutenant 28th	1,150.00	Advanced on account of bounties, &c.
M'Gowan, Johnson, captain 28th infantry	624.00	Advanced on account of bounties, &c.
M'Nair, John, ensign 28th	100.00	Advanced on account of bounties, &c.
Mosby, Benjamin, captain, 28th	1,415.00	Balance on settlement, 7th September, 1820; and reported for suit 28th September, 1820.

STATEMENT--Continued

Names and Rank	Amount Dolls.Cts.	Remarks
Munroe, Jonas, lieutenant	20.00	Advanced on account of bounties, &c.
Melindy, Peter, lieutenant	184.00	Has rendered an account of $183.46, without vouchers.
Morris, David, lieutenant 19th	50.00	Advanced on account of bounties, &c.
M'Cobb, Denny, colonel	890.56	Balance on settlement, 30th January 1816.
Machin, Thomas, captain, 29th	60.00	Advanced on account of quartermaster department.
Morris, Dabney, ensign 20th	262.89	Balance on settlement, 11th December, 1815, $186.10: he is also charged with $76, making this balance.

STATEMENT--Continued

Names and Rank	Amount Dolls.Cts.	Remarks
Madison, George, major militia	644.87	Advanced on account of pay of the army.
Martindale, S. lieutenant colonel militia	200.00	Advanced on account of contingencies.
Marlin, William, ensign New York militia	60.00	Advanced on account of pay of the army.
Magher, Peter, captain militia	200.00	Advanced on account of militia.
Montgomery, Lemuel P. major	229.33	Advanced on account of clothing, and camp equipage, &c.
Maltbie, B. lieutenant	87.63	Advanced on account of bounties, &c.
M'Clelland, Hugh, lieutenant, 32d	384.54	Accounts rendered without vouchers for $127.
Matson, Aaron, Junr. ensign 51st	360.00	Accounts rendered without vouchers for $144.17.
M'Clintock, John, captain Pennsylvania volunteers	794.00	Advanced on account of pay of the army and subsistence.
Miles, William, lieutenant, 43d	428.00	Balance on settlement, 1st April, 1815, $298, and $150 since brought to his debt.
Mebane, Robert, junr.	200.00	Advanced on account of bounties, &c.
Myrick, William, lieutenant	115.51	Balance on settlement, 16th April, 1816.
Madison, William S. surgeon's mate	81.00	Advanced on account of contingencies.
Magruder, Samuel W. surgeon's mate	28.74	Balance on settlement, 25th July 1814.
M'Donald, John, paymaster Ohio militia	3,879.02	Balance on settlement, 28th July, 1820. Suspensions requiring proper vouchers, $217.42.
Morris, Lemuel, captain sea fencibles	2,282.79	Balance on settlement, 7th March, 1820.
Minor, James, lieutenant, 35th	200.00	Account rendered, without vouchers for $56.
Moore, Jeffries H. quartermaster militia	120.00	Advanced on account of quartermaster department.
Macomb, William	250.00	Advanced on account of quartermaster department.
Magruder, James A. Qr. Master detach. Columb. Militia	700.00	Advanced on account of fortifications and quartermaster department.
M'Dowell, James, lieutenant 3d riflemen	1,210.00	Advanced on account of contingencies.
Minton, H. H. lieutenant 7th	32.52	Advanced on account of contingencies, for the transportation of his baggage.
Moses, Philip, ensign 4th infantry	450.00	Advanced on account of bounties and contingencies.
Martin, John, lieutenant 44th	569.25	Accounts rendered, without vouchers for $100.75.
M'Clellan, D. assistant deputy quartermaster general	1.05	Advanced on account of quartermaster department.
Morris, John, captain, 4th riflemen	107.78	Balance on settlement, 21st September, 1816. Suspensions of $104.66.
Mather, George	2,000.00	Advanced on account of contingencies.
M'Intosh, I. S.	58.08	Advanced on account of contingencies, for the transportation of his baggage.
Mills, John, ensign, 37th	589.86	Balance on settlement, 1st October, 1816.

STATEMENT--Continued

Names and Rank	Amount Dolls.Cts.	Remarks
M'Cormick, Samuel, captain	15.00	On account of quartermaster department, for sundry old wagon wheels sold him at fort Jennings, by Josiah Dillon, assistant deputy quartermaster general.
M'Clure, George, major general militia	502.14	Advanced him on account of contingencies.
M'Dowell, James G.	100.00	Advanced on account of bounties, &c.
Mathews, Timothy, ensign 30th	130.00	Advanced on account of bounties, &c.
M'Comas, I. H. quartermaster militia	2,600.00	Advanced on account of militia.

STATEMENT--Continued

Names and Rank	Amount Dolls.Cts.	Remarks
Mott, Sylvanus, lieutenant 29th	100.00	Accounts and vouchers rendered, upon which he claims a balance.
Maxwell, James, ensign 17th	500.00	Advanced on account of bounties, pay, and contingencies.
Mershon, John, ensign 17th	640.00	Account rendered, without vouchers for $157.85
M'Intosh, I. general militia	1,000.00	Advanced on account of contingencies.
Maddox, Town De., lieutenant 24th	100.00	Advanced on account of bounties, &c.
M'Millan, William, lieutenant colonel 17th	637.37	Balance on settlement, 19th November, 1816. Suspensions $68.19.
Munson, Jeremiah R. major 27th	17,685.00	Balance on settlement, 25th September, 1819; and reported for suit 27th September, 1819.
M'Millan, David, lieutenant	900.00	Advanced on account of bounties, contingencies, and quartermaster department.
Moore, Hugh, captain 19th	5.40	Balance on settlement, 25th August, 1818.
Merry, Joseph, ensign 25th	58.60	Balance on settlement, 27th March, 1817. Suspensions $66.15.
Manning, Lawrence, major	2,276.06	Balance on settlement, 12th November, 1819, $3176.6, and reported for suit 24th November, 1819. Suspensions $100. Has since received credit for $900.
Miles, Joseph I. captain 44th	98.00	do. do. 8th August, 1817. Arising from suspensions.
Malcolm, R. M. major 13th	2,906.10	do. do. 25th do. 1820. Suspensions amounting to $430.56, and reported for suit 28th September, 1820.
M'Donald, James, major riflemen	16.41	do. do. 17th May, 1820.
M'Mahon, James, captain	139.00	Advanced on account of quartermaster department.
Morse, Eli B. captain	3,537.26	Balance on settlement, 1st November, 1817, $2921.26. Suspensions $1830.17, and he has since received $616, making this balance.
Morgan, Asa, captain dragoons,	234.65	do. do. 6th November, 1818. Suspensions $98.40.
M'Gowan, Johnston, captain, 28th	2,724.00	Advanced on account of bounties and contingencies.
Meldrum, John, lieutenant 28th	582.00	Advanced on account of bounties, &c.
Munday, James, lieutenant 2d riflemen	279.75	Balance on settlement, 26th August, 1817. Suspensions more than balance.
M'Rae, D. F. ensign 3d riflemen	888.00	do. do. 21st May, 1818. Suspensions $58.
Miller, Abraham, lieutenant artillery	95.00	do. do. 15th December, 1818. Suspensions $8.
Mayre, Robert V. lieutenant	231.96	do. do. 24th July, 1818. Suspensions $191.21.
Manning, Enoch, lieutenant 40th	432.71	do. do 3d July, 1817. Suspensions $12.45.
M'Comb, Joseph, lieutenant	52.50	do. do. 5th July, 1817. Suspensions $2.50
Morrison, Joseph L. captain	834.75	do. do. April, 1820. Suspensions $850.
Maxwell, George, ensign 41st	177.50	Balance on settlement, 12th July, 1817. Suspensions $48.

STATEMENT--Continued

Names and Rank	Amount Dolls.Cts.	Remarks
Mitchell, John, lieutenant corps artillery	177.50	do. do. do. do. Suspensions $159.30
M'Elroy, James F captain 16th	304.52	do. do. do. 1820. Claims credit for $126.11, for which there is no vouchers.
Martin, John B. lieutenant, 38th	60.00	Advanced on account of contingencies.
M'Arthur, Duncan, brigadier general	2,855.16	Accounts rendered without vouchers, upon which he claims a balance.
Melville, Thomas, superintendent public buildings	17,933.84	Balance on settlement, 12th August, 1817, and reported for suit 20th October, 1819.

Names and Rank	Amount Dolls.Cts.	Remarks
M'Kenney, James, lieutenant 22d	57.50	Balance on settlement, 2d September, 1818.
Massey, M. S. lieutenant 2d artillery	632.48	do. do. 14th August, 1818, $339.48. He is charged with $293 in addition thereto, making this balance.
M'Ilvain, D. lieutenant 32d	1,566.00	Advanced on account of bounties and contingencies.
Murdock, Francis B. captain, 32d	1,235.07	Balance on settlement, 20th April, 1820.
M'Laughlin, N. captain light artillery	1,466.32	do. do. 20th July, 1820, arising from suspensions.
Means, Robert, ensign 5th infantry	1,700.00	Advanced on account of bounties and contingencies.
Meyers, Jacob, lieutenant 13th	2,936.00	Balance on settlement, 13th June, 1818.
M'Intire, Aaron, ensign, 23d	703.33	do. do. 26th August, 1817. Suspensions $606.
M'Donald, Angus, lieutenant	1,933.38	do. do. 2d July, 1819. Suspensions $129.23.
Mitchell, George E. colonel	150.00	do. do. 21 October, 1818.
Madison, Andrew L. captain, 12th	324.00	Advanced on account of bounties and pay of the army. Reported for suit.
M'Laughlin, George, lieutenant, 20th	3,282.00	Advanced on account of bounties and contingencies.
Mahon, Thomas, ensign 16th	950.16	Balance on settlement, 1st October, 1818. Suspensions $391.62.
M'Carty, John, lieutenant 23d	343.89	do. do. 2d do. 1818. Suspensions $73.50.
Movers, Benjamin H. lieutenant 33d	470.34	do. do. 15th do. 1817. Suspensions $486.37.
Montgomery, Elijah, captain, 7th	640.38	do. do. 12th May, 1820.
Marston, M. major 5th	88.00	do. do. 22d October, 1819.
Morris, George N. captain light artillery	115.17	do. do. 22d December, 1818.
Mills, William G. lieutenant 14th	298.33	do. do. 26th November, 1817
Mather, John, lieutenant, 2d infantry	2,150.00	do. do. 11th September, 1820, and reported for suit 26th September, 1820.
Machesney, John, captain 16th	688.74	do. do. 17th May, 1820. Suspensions $40.21.
Meline, Florant, lieutenant 15th	189.88	do. do. 10th December, 1817. Suspensions $67.
Melvine, George W. Captain light artillery	3,079.63	do. do. 18th May, 1818. He is also charged with $2,187.55, making a balance of
Marshall, Josiah H. lieutenant Penns. Volunteers	640.00	Advanced on account of volunteers.
Moore, Nimrod H. captain and paymaster 17th	30,098.00	Balance on settlement of his recruiting account, 25th February, 1820, $5777.88, and on account of pay. Has rendered accounts without vouchers $529.12. Reported for suit.
M'Ilhenney, A. captain	2,000.00	Advanced him on account of bounties, &c.
M'Donah, Patrick, lieutenant artillery	504.00	Balance on settlement, 15th September, 1819.
Meyer, Henry, ensign 6th	2,812.00	Has rendered accounts without vouchers for $581.
M'Clure, Joseph, paymaster bat. N. York militia	5,511.75	Balance on settlement, 23d March, 1818.

STATEMENT--Continued

Names and Rank	Amount Dolls.Cts.	Remarks
Miller, James, brigadier general	377.50	Balance on settlement, 23d March, 1818.
Masters, I. E. A. captain 6th	650.00	Advanced on account of bounties and contingencies.
M'Clelland, Robert S. paymaster 8th	8,990.57	Balance on settlement, 17th December, 1818. Reported for suit 17th December, 1818.
Merritt, Joseph E. assistant deputy paymaster	15,213.10	Balance on settlement; and suits instituted against the sureties.

Names and Rank	Amount Dolls.Cts.	Remarks
M'Rea, Farquhar, paymaster 10th infantry	1,273.76	Balance on settlement, 26th August, 1819, and reported for suit, 30th September, 1820.
Maul, John, lieutenant and quartermaster	87.42	do do 8th July, 1818.
M'Donald, William	742.76	do do 2d January, 1819, $502.01; and he has also been charged with $127.75, making this balance.
M'Queen, William, captain	798.88	do do 15th October, 1818
Murphey, John, ensign 13th	821.00	do do 23d May, 1818, and reported for suit, 27th September, 1820. This whole amount arising from suspensions.
Martin, Beverly, lieutenant 8th	706.24	do do 25th February, 1819. Suspensions $78.11.
M'Clain, Joseph, lieutenant riflemen	866.00	Accounts rendered without vouchers for $224.
Morrison, James, paymaster Georgia militia	9,000.00	By letter of the 17th October, 1820, promises to send on his accounts immediately by mail.
Mills, Peter, major 23d	1,878.53	Balance on settlement, 2d July, 1818. Suspensions and items not admissible to the amount of this balance.
M'Farland, A. lieutenant 2d dragoons	50.00	Advanced on account of contingencies.
M'Chain, George, lieutenant 25th	750.00	Advanced on account of quartermaster department, hospital, and contingencies.
Morgan, Lodowick, captain riflemen	5,438.54	Balance on settlement, 29th October, 1819. and reported for suit, 10th November, 1819.
M'Farland, Daniel, major 23d	947.00	do do 11th September, 1820, and reported for suit, 26th September, 1820.
Maxwell, Thompson, captain	62.00	Advanced on account of quartermaster department.
Morse, William S. lieutenant 9th	1,479.55	Balance on settlement, 14th December, 1819.
Millikin, Joel, captain 33d	691.46	do do 21st July, 1818. Suspensions $66; and reported for suit, 17th October, 1820.
Mountford, John, lieutenant artillery	686.00	Advanced on account of quartermaster department, and bounties, &c.
Morgan, Zacquill, captain 12th	459.00	Balance on settlement, 22d July, 1818.
Martin, James, lieutenant dragoons	750.00	Accounts rendered; apparent balance due, $546.50.
M'Intosh, John N. captain light artillery	265.10	Balance on settlement, 23d March, 1819.
Moulton, Josiah, captain 33d	466.39	do do 17th April, 1820. Suspensions $67.29; and reported for suit, 17th October, 1820.
Mooney, William, captain, 22d	340.25	do do 8th August, 1818. Suspensions $112.
Mason, John, captain 28th	2,100.39	do do 15th do. Suspensions $472.75; and reported for suit, 27th Sept. 1820.

STATEMENT--Continued

Names and Rank	Amount Dolls.Cts.			Remarks
Mead, Hodijah, captain 20th	1,215.12	do	do	21st do.
Morgan, Thomas I. ensign 17th	390.55	do	do	25th do. Suspensions $278.50.
Miller, Edward W. lieutenant 2d rifle	16.98	do	do	27th do. Suspensions $12.
M'Clelland, Mathew W. lieutenant 39th infantry	491.00	do	do	30th May, 1820. Suspensions $42; and states that the sum of $448 was stolen from him.
Morrow, James, lieutenant 22d	31.41	do	do	19th April, 1820.
Mytenger, George, ensign 22d	272.85	do	do	4th September, 1818.
Miller, Jacob, captain 7th	192.17	do	do	16th do. Suspensions $223.75.
Mitchell, Richard, ensign 17th	626.00	do	do	17th do. $176. He is also charged with $450, making this balance.
M'Clure, Joseph, lieutenant 34th	610.42	do	do	18th do. Suspensions $124.31. Reported for suit, 17th October, 1820.

Names and Rank	Amount Dolls.Cts.	Remarks
Moore, James F. lieutenant 28th	200.00	Balance on settlement, 19th September, 1818.
Merrill, John, lieutenant 31st	78.32	do do 28th do.
Montgomery, William W. paymaster Georgia militia	3,077.50	do do 11th July, 1820.
M'Gaw, Richard, paymaster 7th	566.49	do do 23d October, 1818
Milligan, John, lieutenant 19th	550.62	do do 27th November, 1818. Suspensions $552.47.
Moore, Thomas P. captain 12th	49.07	do do 10th do 1819.
Monroe, Thomas	52.98	Advanced on account of contingencies.
Martin, Hugh R. captain	300.00	Advanced on account of bounties, &c.
Meigs, Return J. late governor of Ohio	52,297.69	Accounts and vouchers rendered upon which he claims a balance. Not yet examined.
M'Cloud, Collin, lieutenant 26th	669.00	Vouchers rendered for $596.
Morrow, William, paymaster 2d Ohio militia	5,985.08	Balance on settlement, 30th December, 1818, $15,997.08. Suspensions $545. Has since received credit for $9,994, leaving this balance.
M'Keeham, surgeon's mate Ohio militia	65.00	Advanced on account of medical and hospital department.
Meed, James, captain 17th	131.24	Balance on settlement, 12th August, 1817. He is also charged with $100, making this balance.
M'Knight, Alexander, lieutenant 29th	120.02	do do 11th January, 1819. Suspensions $8.
Martin, Wyley, captain	868.24	do. do 31st March, 1819, $1,175.59; has since received credit for $305.35, leaving this balance. Suspensions $319.43.
Meredith, John L. ensign and quartermaster	223.07	do do 18th March, 1819, $136.57; he is also charged with $86.58, making this balance.
Marlin, Ralph, major 22d	5,032.19	do do 28th September, 1819, and reported for suit 5th October, 1819.
Mann, John G. ensign 25th	86.00	do do 7th January, 1820.
Minor, Asa, ensign 20th	72.20	do do 24th April, 1819. Suspensions $21.
Mullikin, David, captain, 22d	19.23	do do 16th May, 1820. Suspensions $9.22.
Mountjoy, Thomas, lieutenant 17th	220.00	Advanced on account of bounties, pay, and contingencies.
M'Donald, John, colonel U. S. army	16.41	Balance on settlement, 14th March, 1820.
M'Fadden, Neal, lieutenant 19th infantry	538.28	Do do 17th May, 1819. Suspensions, 458 dollars.
M'Lain, Isaac, paymaster Virginia militia	385.22	Do do 17th May, 1819.
Morris, Robert, ensign 15th	234.16	Do do 24th June, 1819. Suspensions, $209.80.
M'Laughlin Edward, late D. paymaster	3,342.21	Do do 26th June, 1819.
Mitchell, John, agent for prisoners of war	674.00	Do do 21st September, 1819.

STATEMENT--Continued

Names and Rank	Amount Dolls.Cts.	Remarks
Merrill, John, paymaster 34th	1,418.86	Do do 14th July, 1819. Reported for suit, 3d October, 1820.
Miltenberger, Anthony, captain, 38th	196.75	Do do 29th July, 1819. Suspensions, 9 dollars 12 cents.
M'Lean, John, to pay Ohio militia	8,169.81	Vouchers rendered; payments not completed; will pay over the balance.
M'Dougal, John, paymaster Ohio militia	16,811.01	Balance on settlement, 28th February, 1820.
M'Laughlin, James, to pay Virginia militia	376.55	Advanced on account of pay and subsistence.
M'Clelland, M. lieutenant 7th	200.00	Advanced on account of bounties, &c.

STATEMENT--Continued

Names and Rank	Amount Dolls.Cts.	Remarks
M'Neil, Archibald F. lieutenant colonel light dragoons	5,000.00	Advanced , in 1813, to purchase horses for the light dragoons.
M'Ilvain, John, lieutenant 26th	119.50	Balance on settlement, 16th September, 1819. Suspensions, 144 dollars.
Marshall, Joseph, lieutenant 14th	28.00	Advanced on account of pay of the army.
M'Nish, Henry, South Carolina militia	703.34	On account of pay.
Morrill, Joseph, captain, 31st	58.40	Balance on settlement, 25th August, 1818., 8 dollars 40 cents; he is also charged with 50 dollars, on account of bounties, &c making this balance.
M'Closkey, James, captain, &c.	5,515.40	Balance on settlement, 29th October, 1819, and reported for suit, 5th November, 1819.
Martin, Wait, lieutenant 23d	276.00	Do do 26th November, 1819. Suspensions, 106 dollars.
Myers, Isaac, ensign 16th	678.00	Do do 29th November, 1819. Suspensions, 182 dollars.
Morris, William, jr. lieutenant 33d	369.14	Do do 4th December, 1819. Suspensions, 319 dollars.
M'Cally, Alexander, lieutenant 33d	140.34	Do do 20th do 1819.Suspensions, 130 dollars.
M'Clelland, John, captain, 3d infantry	1,571.57	Do do 13th do 1819; and reported for suit, 28th February, 1820.
M'Cluney, John, major 23d	2,530.50	Reported for suit, 10th November, 1819.
Meller, George P. Kentucky militia	46,422.42	Accounts on file, and under examination.
Moss, Benjamin W. Virginia militia	40,250.00	Accounts on file, and under examination.
Martin, Olephant	35.50	No accounts received.
Mitchell, Samuel H. lieutenant, 29th infantry	125.00	No accounts received.
Martin, John, lieutenant 16th	570.00	No accounts received.
Mitchell, Charles, lieutenant 13th	90.00	Has rendered his accounts and vouchers.
Nash, William A. lieutenant 34th	68.00	Balance on settlement, 21st December, 1814, $48. He is also charged with $200; making this balance.
Nevers, William, lieutenant 34th	379.09	Accounts rendered, without vouchers, for $194.18.
Nash, John, ensign, 34th	78.57	Accounts rendered, without vouchers, for $45.91.
Newbegin, George, lieutenant 33d	12.80	Balance on settlement, 27th July, 1814.
Nelson, George, captain	850.00	Advanced on account of bounties and contingencies.
Nearing, Asahel, captain 19th	1,104.58	Balance on settlement, 24th January, 1814, $389.58. He has since been charged with $715; making this balance.
Neville, Presley I. lieutenant artillery	750.00	Accounts rendered for 12 dollars.
Nye, Samuel, major 3d infantry	1,096.17	Balance on settlement, 28th June, 1815, $566.17. He is also charged $530; making this balance.
Norvell, Joshua, lieutenant	60.00	Advanced on account of bounties, &c.
Newman, Montgomery, lieutenant 2d artillery	100.00	Advanced on account of bounties, &c.

STATEMENT--Continued

Names and Rank	Amount Dolls.Cts.	Remarks
Nicholes, George, surgeon's mate	20.00	Advanced on account of contingencies.
Noble, Ransom, major	200.00	Advanced on account of militia.
Nash, Martin, military agency	20.00	Advanced on account of militia.
Norton, C. A. lieutenant, 26th	200.00	Advanced on account of bounties, &c.
Nerrill, Robert, lieutenant 26th	560.00	Advanced on account of bounties, &c. and contingencies.

STATEMENT--Continued

Names and Rank	Amount Dolls.Cts.	Remarks
Nickerson, Freeman, lieutenant 31st	320.00	Balance on settlement, 26th September, 1820; and reported for suit.
Nicholson, John, captain sea fencibles	240.00	Advanced on account of contingencies.
Noyes, Christopher, lieutenant, 15th	25.00	Advanced on account of quartermaster department.
Neal, Francis, quartermaster 36th	100.00	Advanced on account of quartermaster department.
Neely, Nicholas, ensign 19th	300.00	Advanced on account of bounties, &c.
Neal, Robert, lieutenant, 40th	230.60	Balance on settlement, 11th September, 1816.
Nelson, William, ensign, 17th	1,104.00	Do do 14th March, 1820. By his letter of 19th May, 1820, promises to render his accounts in three months.
Nicholas, Carey, captain, 7th infantry	817.92	Balance on settlement, 19th February, 1817, $360. He is also charged with other moneys, making this sum.
Nelson, Joseph S. captain 36th infantry	1,970.00	Account rendered on which he claim $50, he has received moneys not yet brought to his debit, leaving an apparent balance of $2245. States that he has lost all his vouchers.
Norman, William H. lieutenant, 43d	687.24	Balance on settlement 2d May, 1817. Suspensions $279.98.
Nicholas, William, captain 2d artillery	4,717.38	Do. do. 28th June, 1815, $159.38; he is also charged with $4,558, making this balance due by him. He has rendered an Account for bounties and premiums. Dead and insolvent.
Nicholas, Robert C.	209.06	Do. do. 29th September, 1815.
Norton, Eliker, lieutenant	40.00	Advanced on account of bounties and pay.
Norton, Lambert, lieutenant 1st riflemen	44.07	Balance on settlement, 20th January, 1818. Suspensions to a greater amount than this balance.
Northup, Henry, captain	4,292.00	Has rendered vouchers for $1,100, and states that he has additional accounts and vouchers to render.
Newcomb, Smith, ensign 29th	2,431.93	Balance on settlement, 8th August, 1818.
Noland, Benjamin, paymaster Maryland militia	2,649.00	Do. do. 15th July, 1820.
Neilson, D. apothecary general	550.00	Advanced on account of medical and hospital department.
Newkirk, Charles, lieutenant artillery	50.00	Advanced on account of quartermaster department and contingencies.
Norris, Lewis, ensign 9th	189.14	Balance on settlement, 22d October, 1816, $89.14. Suspensions $24. He is also charged with $100, leaving this balance.
Neilson, Archibald, lieutenant 7th	865.50	Do. do. 29th July, 1818. Suspensions 1,060.12.
Neil, Adam, lieutenant 2d artillery	76.98	Do. do. 7th September, 1818. Suspensions $77.
Neilson, Oliver H. lieutenant 38th	27.25	Do. do. 6th October, 1818, arising from suspensions.
Nelson, Alton, lieutenant 29th	199.22	Do. do. 19th November, 1818.
Neale, Henry C. captain 36th	902.19	Do. do. 16th April, 1819. Has rendered additional vouchers for $307.92 and claims a balance for pay.

STATEMENT--Continued

Names and Rank	Amount Dolls.Cts.	Remarks
Neale, James, lieutenant	600.00	Advanced on account of bounties, &c.
Noble, Andrew, paymaster 2d Pennsylvania militia	218.81	Balance on settlement, 24th April 1819.
Nourse, Charles J. Major	873.71	Do.　　do.　　　29th April, 1819. Suspensions $800.95, and has rendered additional papers.
Nicholson, Benjamin, lieutenant, 14th	457.67	Do.　　do.　　　5th May, 1819. Suspensions $61.
Nash, James, New York militia	21,500.00	Accounts on file and under examination.

STATEMENT--Continued

Names and Rank	Amount Dolls.Cts.	Remarks
Noble, John, lieutenant 7th	250.00	Advanced on account of bounties, &c.
Nesbit, Alexander, paymaster North Carolina militia	582.05	Balance on settlement 16th July, 1819. Reported for suit, 20th October, 1820.
Nye, John, captain 19th	142.39	Do. do. 21st December, 1819. Suspensions $6, and claims credit $17.78, for which no vouchers are produced.
Norton, Edward, ensign	572.25	Advanced on account of bounties, pay and contingencies. Reported for suit.
Nicholas, John Jun. lieutenant	130.00	Balance on settlement, 24th August, 1820. Reported for suit 20th September, 1820
Norris, James F., lieutenant 9th	435.83	Do. do. 15th May, 1820. Suspensions $174.15. Reported for suit.
Oldham, Richard, captain 7th	416.80	Advanced on account of bounties, &c. and camp equipage, &c.
Overton, William H. captain	1,025.13	Balance on settlement, 21st August, 1816, $830.61. He is also charged With $194.52, making this balance.
Orme, Jonathan brigadier general Vermont militia	1,558.75	Advanced on account of quartermaster department and contingencies.
O'Neal, Ferdinand A. lieutenant sea fencibles	10.00	Advanced on account of contingencies.
O'Connor, John, surgeon's mate	20.00	No accounts rendered.
Ogden, Peter V., captain volunteers	350.00	Advanced on account of quartermaster department.
Oglevie, Peter Jun. captain, 13th	692.60	Balance on settlement, 27th January, 1820m $292.60. He is subsequently charged with $400, making his balance. Has rendered additional accounts and vouchers.
Olmstead, Edward, lieutenant 15th	471.65	Do. do. 14th April, 1817. Suspensions $242.
Owens, Joseph, lieutenant 43d	12,335.03	Do. do. 15th July, 1819. Reported for suit 3d October, 1820.
Oliver, Joseph, lieutenant 43d	393.91	Do. do. 20th December, 1819. arising from suspensions.
Ormsby, Mason, major	216.00	Accounts and vouchers rendered on which he claims a balance.
Ogden, Benjamin, S. captain 3d artillery	4,716.00	Balance on settlement 13th December, 1819. Reported for suit 28th February, 1820.
Odell, Azariah, lieutenant 23d	72.74	Do. do. 1st October, 1817. Suspensions $18.
Osgood, Lemuel H. lieutenant 43d	270.00	Advanced on account of quartermaster department.
Orr & Greely, contractors under contract 10 March , 1817	31,180.98	Balance on a statement made by the 3d Auditor, 18th October, 1819; now before the 2d Comptroller for decision.
Owings, Thomas D. colonel 28th	7,684.91	Do. do. 28th March, 1815, $1,284.91. He is also charged with $6,400. making this balance.
Oliver, William, assistant deputy quartermaster general	1,542.97	Do. do. 25th July, 1818.

STATEMENT--Continued

Names and Rank	Amount Dolls.Cts.	Remarks
Overton, Thomas J. lieutenant and quartermaster 17th	1,146.01	Do. do. 20 July, 1819. Suspensions $366.68.
Ord, James, lieutenant 38th	500.00	Do. do. 23d September, 1818.
Oliver, Matthew, New York militia	31.97	Accounts on file and under examination. Audited 14th November, 1820, and balance due U. States $31.97.
Orr, Alexander D. assistant deputy quartermaster gen.	2,631.49	Advanced on account of quartermaster department.
Owens, Samuel, paymaster 6th Maryland militia	121.72	Balance on settlement 2d March, 1819.
Owens, Simon, captain 1st infanty	639.13	Balance on settlement, 10th October, 1811, $439.13. He is also charged with $200 on account of bounties, &c., making this balance.
Pierce, Leonard, lieutenant 34th	600.00	Advanced on account of bounties, &c.
Plummer, Richard, lieutenant 10th	610.00	Account rendered without vouchers for $133, leaving an apparent balance of $477.

STATEMENT--Continued

Names and Rank	Amount Dolls.Cts.	Remarks
Phinney, G. G. lieutenant	100.00	Advanced on account of bounties, &c.
Peckham, Paul, ensign 4th	1,128.00	Account rendered without vouchers, for $1,021.60. He has received other moneys, not yet brought to his debit. Apparent balance, $306.40.
Pifer, Peter, lieutenant artillery	110.84	Balance on settlement, 3d June, and 6th August 1814, $20.87. He is also charged with $90, making this balance.
Peyton, Bernard, captain 20th	76.51	Advanced on account of bounties and contingencies.
Parlin, Josiah, ensign 34th	450.00	Balance on settlement, 5th August, 1820. Reported for suit, 26th September, 1820.
Pindergrast, G. E. hospital surgeon	.20	Do. do. 15th July, 1814.
Patterson, Thomas A. lieu. & last assis. Military agent	162.40	Advanced on account of camp equipage. $12.40. It being a balance due by him out of moneys advanced by William Linnard, on the settlement of Linnard's account, and $150 on account of recruiting purposes.
Pasteur, Edward colonel	50.50	Balance due on settlement, 17th May, 1811.
Pennell, William, captain 6th	10.00	Advanced on account of camp equipments, &c.
Plume, John J. lieutenant and quartermaster 6th	280.00	Advanced on account of bounties, &c.
Peyton, James R.	200.00	Advanced on account of bounties, &c.
Parker, Thomas, captain	184.00	Advanced on account of bounties, &c.
Parker, William, lieutenant 3d riflemen	318.02	Balance on settlement, 24th July, 1815.
Pach, David, lieutenant 5th	500.00	Advanced on account of quartermaster department.
Paulding, William K. ensign 24th	524.96	Balance on settlement, 11th March, 1816, $388. He is also chargeable with $136.98, making this balance.
Pitts, Thomas, captain	32.00	Advanced on account of quartermaster department.
Palmer, Aaron, captain militia	100.00	Advanced on account of militia.
Porter, Peter B. quartermaster general	11,391.00	Balance on settlement, 24th March, 1820. He has claims to nearly this amount, which have been suspended for further vouchers.
Phagan, John, captain 39th	2,804.00	Balance on settlement, 18th February, 1820. Suspensions, $1,313.74
Paige, Daniel, lieutenant	508.00	Advanced on account of bounties, &c.
Putnam, John, lieutenant 31st	310.00	Advanced on account of bounties and contingencies.
Presser, William, lieutenant 7th	280.00	Advanced on account of bounties, pay, and contingencies.
Price, Samuel, captain artillery	587.83	Accounts rendered without vouchers, upon which he claims credit for $365.50, making this balance.
Payne, James, captain Virginia militia	14.93	Balance on settlement, 30th August, 1820.
Pike, James, lieutenant 4th infantry	200.00	Advanced on account of bounties, &c.

STATEMENT--Continued

Names and Rank	Amount Dolls.Cts.	Remarks
Parker, Philip S. judge advocate	100.00	Advanced on account of quartermaster department.
Pegram, Robert, lieutenant colonel 35th	800.00	Advanced on account of bounties, &c.
Pettibone, Chauncey, lieutenant 6th	70.00	Advanced on account of contingencies.
Parmell, Giles H. lieutenant 37th	80.00	Accounts and vouchers rendered, upon which he claims a balance.
Pinney, Abner P. captain 27th	500.00	Advanced on account of bounties, &c.

STATEMENT--Continued

Names and Rank	Amount Dolls.Cts.	Remarks
Phelps, Matthew, major	1,519.04	Balance on settlement, 27th April, 1816.
Price, Richard, lieutenant 7th	100.00	Advanced on account of bounties, &c.
Prichard, William, captain 2d riflemen	869.31	Balance on settlement, 2d September, 1816, $569.31. Suspensions, $568.04. He is also charged with 300 dollars, making this balance.
Paul, George, colonel 19th	542.33	Do. do. 6th March, 1819.
Pierce, Henry D. major 44th	2,073.72	Do. do. 8th December, 1819; and reported for suit 28th February, 1820.
Price, Philip P. lieutenant 19th	2,081.00	Do. do. 9th do do do do.
Patterson, B. M. lieutenant 39th	1,000.00	Advanced on account of bounties, &c.
Porter, Thomas C.	115.00	Advanced on account of bounties and contingencies.
Payne, John C. assis. Deputy quartermaster general	2,219.77	Balance on settlement, 12th October, 1819. Suspensions $1,559.79, and reported for suit.
Paycock, William, major 39th	1,100.00	Advanced on account of bounties, &c.
Pemberton, John T. Dist. Paymaster	1,256,924.60	Accounts and vouchers rendered, and under examination, upon which he claims a balance.
Poland, Benjamin, captain, 34th	120.00	Advanced on account of bounties and pay of the army.
Paige, John K. captain, 13th	878.36	Balance on settlement, 22d August, 1818.
Palmer, Loring, captain 9th	150.00	Advanced on account of bounties, &c.
Porter, George W. lieutenant 18th	53.18	Balance on settlement, 21st July, 1818. Suspensions $97.56.
Piatt, James, lieutenant 15th	1,225.87	Do. do. April 1816, $1125.87. He is since charged with $100. Suspensions $204.
Preston, James P. colonel	2,740.00	Advanced on account of bounties, pay, and contingencies. By letter of 16th December, 1819, he states, his papers were deranged, and nearly destroyed on Lake Ontario, but will attend to the settlement of his accounts.
Page, Charles, captain, 29th	1,209.36	Balance on settlement, 12th September, 1817; suspensions $46.
Palmer, Barnabas, lieutenant, 23d	832.50	Do. do. 5th August, 1818. Suspensions, $295.30
Pike, Zebulon M brigadier general	991.34	Do. do. 13th June, 1820.
Pendleton, John, lieutenant 3d riflemen	84.85	Do. do. 3d November, 1817.
Philips, Joseph, captain 2d artillery	249.08	Do. do. 24th March, 1820.
Peters, George P. paymaster 4th infantry	1,122.73	Do. do. 12th January, 1819.
Phelps, Samuel S. paymaster militia	389.28	Do. do. 24th October, 1820. Suspensions $91.52.

STATEMENT--Continued

Names and Rank	Amount Dolls.Cts.	Remarks
Phillips, Henry, deputy paymaster	15,600.58	Do. do. 25th April, 1818, $15,601.82; reported for suit: he has since received credit of $1.24.
Post, Ezra, captain	90.75	Do. do. 15th December, 1819. Suspensions 12 dollars.
Porter, Moses, brigadier general	11.45	Do. do. 21st May, 1818.
Piatt, John H. contractor	48,230.77	An additional sum of $12,855.37 is chargeable to his account, and credits have been allowed by the 2d comptroller, under the act passed for his relief; exhibiting a balance in his favor, which will be entered when the balance is paid.
Pratt, John, lieutenant 31st	157.28	Balance on settlement, 27th January, 1819. arising from suspensions.
Powers, Thomas M. lieutenant and paymaster 16th	2,984.59	Do. do. 19th July and 3d April 1820. Has claims for suspended vouchers.

Names and Rank	Amount Dolls.Cts.	Remarks
Purdy, Robert, colonel 4th	60.00	Advanced on account of bounties, &c.
Pelham, Peter, lieutenant 21st	606.38	Balance on settlement, 20th May, 1818. Suspensions 72 dollars.
Prince, Joseph P. captain artillery	7,516.33	Do. do. 14th October, 1819. Suspensions 12 dollars.
Puthuff, William H. captain	10,136.36	Advanced on account of bounties, contingencies, and quartermaster department.
Perkins, S. M. ensign 31st	580.00	Account rendered without vouchers for #30.28; apparent balance $549.72.
Peabody, Asa	130.00	Advanced on account of bounties and contingencies.
Procktor, Charles, captain 21st	851.32	Balance on settlement, 26th February, 1817. Suspensions $88.49.
Peters, Charles, lieutenant 44th	818.50	Do. do. 20th June, 1818. Suspensions $541.50.
Peters, Thomas R. paymaster 1st Penna. Volunteers	4,295.44	Do. do. 2d August, 1820. Suspensions $75.75.
Pendleton, William F. ensign 20th	470.19	Do. do. 29th June, 1818. Suspensions $93.95.
Price, Benjamin, ensign	50.00	Advanced on account of quartermaster department.
Pendleton, James T. Kentucky militia	29,472.79	Accounts rendered, and under examination.
Parker, Philip J. major	50.00	Advance on account of quartermaster department.
Porter, James M. captain Virginia militia	64.91	Balance on settlement, 13th April, 1819.
Pettibone, John R. ensign 30th	49.40	Do. do. 11th July, 1818. Suspensions 27 dollars.
Perkins, Joseph, lieutenant 24th	1,280.00	Do. do. 26th October, 1818, $1180. He is also charged with 100 dollars on account of contingencies, making this balance.
Ponnelly, Charles, paymaster New York militia	8,000.00	Written to on the subject, 8th October, 1817. Reported for suit 22d July, 1818.
Peckham, Lewis, lieutenant 4th	103.82	Balance on settlement, 17th July, 1818. Suspensions 41 dollars.
Powers, Levi, captain 21st	176.17	Do. do. 21st do. Suspensions 160 dollars.
Powell, James, lieutenant 33d	144.08	Do. do. 25th do. Suspensions $86.54
Preble, Rufus, lieutenant 4th	295.50	Do do. 27th do.
Pease, George	533.75	On account of subsistence, for sundry hides sold him at Fort Meigs, in 1814.
Patterson, John, ensign 27th	92.00	Balance on settlement, 26th February, 1820
Page, Enoch, lieutenant 45th	4.00	Do. do. 17th August, 1818, arising from suspensions.
Patterson, Reuben B. paymaster	388.58	Do. do. 28th June, 1820.
Proctor, George V. doctor	3,591.50	Advanced on account of medical and hospital department.
Pryor, Nathaniel, captain, 44th	398.00	Balance on settlement, 26th August, 1818, arising from suspensions.
Pagan, Alexander	283.50	Do. do. 28th August, 1818. Suspensions $238.50.
Perry, James, captain 40th	721.56	Do. do. 10th November, 1818. Suspensions $717.56.

STATEMENT--Continued

Names and Rank	Amount Dolls.Cts.		Remarks
Pettipool, Joseph, paymaster 20th	58,699.26	Do.	do. 11th September, 1818. Suspensions $57,409.56. reported for suit, 28th October, 1820: has rendered additional accounts for recruiting purposes.
Paine, Brackett, lieutenant 21st	87.50	Do.	do. 28th September, 1818. Suspensions $28.82.
Pegram, Edward L. lieutenant 35th	763.00	Do.	do. 8th January 1819. Suspensions 448 dollars.
Peek, Adam, ensign 24th	1,293.15	Do.	do. 3d December, 1818, $1097.45. Suspensions $430.23; he is also charged with $1,950.70, making this balance.

STATEMENT--Continued

Names and Rank	Amount Dolls.Cts.	Remarks
Palmer, James, lieutenant 29th	17.75	Balance on settlement, 15th December, 1818.
Price, Clarkson, lieutenant 26th	256.00	Do. do. 16th do. 1818, $126; he is also charged with $130, making this balance.
Pope, Samuel C. lieutenant 40th	5.07	Do. do. 25th February, 1819.
Palmer, Anthony, lieutenant 30th	606.00	Do. do. 18th March, 1819. Suspensions $45.79.
Prevost, Frederick J. lieutenant 6th	240.00	Advanced on account of bounties, &c.
Peyton, Robert, captain 2d infantry	213.55	Balance on settlement, 29th June, 1819.
Perkins, Richard, paymaster 3d Virginia militia	421.00	Balance on settlement, 2d June, 1819.
Pierce, Benjamin K. captain artillery	189.00	Do do 16th June, 1819.
Perley, John, lieutenant 9th	746.39	Do do 18th September, 1819.
Porter, William R. paymaster 7th Virginia militia	864.54	Do do 18th January, 1820. Suspensions and disallowances, which he promises to remove, and requests time to petition Congress.
Provost, Lewis M. paymaster Pennsylvania militia	1,608.32	Balance on settlement, 21st October, 1820. Suspensions $62.95.
Phillips, John W. paymaster South Carolina militia	857.83	Do do 18th July, 1820. Suspensions, $126.09.
Pugh, Jonathan, paymaster Virginia militia	2,259.63	Accounts and vouchers rendered, and apparent balance $18.07.
Price, William, paymaster 14th Kentucky militia	12,765.59	Balance on settlement, 1st August, 1819. Suspensions $3,595.
Perry, David, late 9th	2,000.00	Account rendered without vouchers $111. Apparent balance $1,889.
Perdee, Abraham, captain 15th	483.16	Balance on settlement, 18th September, 1819.
Packard, N. R. brigade quartermaster	3,000.00	Do do 30th September, 1819, and reported for suit 5th October, 1819.
Phelps, Ephraham L.	1,810.16	Do do 16th January, 1816.
Peebles, Joel, lieutenant 29th	1,000.00	Advanced on account of bounties, &c.
Phillips, Richard, ensign 23d	150.00	Advanced on account of bounties, &c.
Plummer, John H. late deputy commissary	13,775.57	Balance on settlement, 19th October, 1819, and reported for suit, 20th October, 1819.
Pearson, John A. colonel North Carolina militia	2,000.00	He states that he rendered his accounts to quartermaster Champlain for this money. They have never been received at this office.
Parris, Alexander, cap. And superintendent of artificers	1,050.00	Balance on settlement, 8th December, 1819, and reported for suit, 28th February, 1820.
Petre, Jacob D. New York militia	4,757.04	Accounts rendered, and under examination. Adjusted 16th November, 1820; balance due the United States, $370.71.
Quarles, Randolph, lieutenant 39th	4.00	Balance on settlement, 26th March, 1817.
Queen, Nicholas L. citizen of Washington	550.00	Do do 12th September, 1820. Reported for suit, 26th September, 1820.

STATEMENT--Continued

Names and Rank	Amount Dolls.Cts.	Remarks
Quivey, Charles, captain 17th	3,050.00	Do do 8th December, 1819, and reported for suit, 28th February, 1820.
Radcliff, John C. paymaster	175.97	Do do 5th July, 1820.
Rutland, John, captain	160.00	Advanced on account of bounties, &c.
Roberts, John, 3d wagon master	1,353.50	Advanced on account of quartermaster department.
Reed, Phineas, brigade quartermaster	340.00	Advanced on account of quartermaster department.

STATEMENT--Continued

Names and Rank	Amount Dolls.Cts.	Remarks
Russell, Gilbert C captain 7th	357.37	Advanced on account of quartermaster department, and medical and hospital department. It being for sundry claims existing against the quartermaster department by Jno. A. Watson. Late assistant deputy quartermaster general at Mobile, the assignment of which he represents to hold. In consequence, The Secretary of War directed a warrant to issue for the amount.
Rich, Peter, captain militia dragoons	900.00	Advanced on account of quartermaster department.
Roberts, John, captain volunteers	80.00	Advanced on account of pay of the army.
Ragland, James P. Virginia militia	44,832.47	Accounts rendered and under examination.
Roof, Adam J. paymaster New York militia	309.05	Balance on settlement, 11th September, 1820.
Read, James, major	208.24	Advanced on account of quartermaster department.
Read, James, captain artillery	200.00	Advanced on account of bounties, &c.
Root, Richard H. lieutenant 13th	227.70	Balance on settlement, 20th December, 1812, $127. He is also charged with $100, on account of bounties, &c. He has an account and vouchers for $84. Advanced on account of contingencies.
Riddle, John, lieutenant	40.00	Advanced on account of contingencies.
Read, William B. lieutenant 3d artillery	86.50	Balance on settlement, 15th April, and 22d July 1815.
Robertson, Alexander, lieutenant 17th	1,295.00	Advanced on account of bounties, pay and contingencies.
Ritchie, Thomas, lieutenant 36th	100.00	Advanced on account of bounties, &c.
Rhodes, Jonas, ensign 28th	100.00	Advanced on account of bounties, &c.
Ricketts, Benjamin, ensign 14th	50.00	Account rendered, for which he claims a credit for $500. He has received other moneys not yet brought to his debit.
Rouche, Isaac, captain 23d	733.00	Advanced on account of pay of the army
Riffetts, Thomas, lieutenant 20th	2,557.36	Balance on settlement, 17th July, 1815. Reported for suit.
Ricaird, John, paymaster	6,218.62	Do do 20th March, 1816. Insolvent.
Robinson, Samuel, ensign	10.00	Advanced him on account of militia.
Renick, Henry, captain Kentucky militia	360.00	Advanced on account of quartermaster department.
Ragland, Thomas, ensign 3d riflemen	50.00	Advanced on account of contingencies.
Rogers, G. H. ensign	336.24	Do do do
Riding, John T. lieutenant	50.00	Do do do
Robinson, L. lieutenant 26th	467.00	Do do do
Rivers, William, lieutenant 35th	1,600.00	Advanced on account of bounties, &c.
Ross, William, ensign 21st	241.32	Balance on settlement, 12th May, 1820.
Rose, Neil B. brigade quartermaster Tennessee militia	3,650.00	Advanced on account of quartermaster department.

STATEMENT--Continued

Names and Rank	Amount Dolls.Cts.	Remarks
Rose, Daniel, captain	77.50	Advanced on account of quartermaster department.
Richardson, Joseph L. deputy paymaster	3,062.77	Balance on settlement, 6th October, 1820.
Ross, Robert P. lieutenant 27th	720.00	Advanced on account of bounties, &c.
Rawle, William, captain militia cavalry	300.00	Advanced on account of quartermaster department.
Rose, Alexander F. captain 6th	225.00	Advanced on account of contingencies.

STATEMENT--Continued

Names and Rank	Amount Dolls.Cts.	Remarks
Ransham, Henry, lieutenant	508.00	Advanced on account of bounties and contingencies.
Ronalds, Mason, lieutenant, 13th	408.00	Advanced on account of pay of the army, and bounties, &c.
Ruland, Isaac, ensign militia	60.00	Advanced on account of quartermaster department.
Roger, Willis, assistant deputy quartermaster general	1,988.90	Advanced on account of quartermaster department.
Riddle, James W. ensign 14th	203.59	Balance on settlement, 25th September, 1815. Suspensions $145.25.
Rather, John T. lieutenant 7th	143.46	Do. do. 17th May, 1820. Suspensions $245.
Reynolds, Benjamin, captain 39th	743.90	Do. do. 26th March, 1817. Suspensions $70.
Ross, Leonard, captain 40th	49.82	Do. do. 24th July, 1819.
Ross, George T., captain 44th	10,128.77	Do. do. 25th September, 1819. Suspensions $230; and Reported for suit 27th Sept. 1819.
Randolph, Edward B. late 20th infantry	2,248.45	Do. do. 10th August, 1818, $248.45. He is also charged $2,000 on account of quartermaster department.
Riddle, David, major	1,096.00	Advanced on account of contingencies.
Read, Thomas M.	761.11	Balance on settlement, 17th December, 1817, $781.11. Suspensions $51.38. He stands credited for $20 not embraced in the above settlement; leaving this balance.
Rowland, Thomas, major	141.00	Advanced on account of bounties, &c.
Reynolds, John G. lieutenant 28th	220.00	Advanced on account of bounties, &c.
Rhodes, Jonas, ensign 28th	750.00	Advanced on account of bounties and contingencies.
Rich, Peter, lieutenant 14th	635.50	Balance on settlement, 13th April, 1819. Suspensions $35.75.
Reab, George, lieutenant, 13th	2.25	Do. do. 3d July, 1817.
Read, George, lieutenant, 16th	243.16	Do. do. 24th July, 1817. Suspensions $69.50.
Reynolds, T., lieutenant 18th	404.50	Do. do. 26th June, 1817. Suspensions, $124.75
Rivery, Peter, late deputy commissary	172.90	Do. do. 18th February, 1818.
Read, William M. lieutenant 2d artillery	8.63	Do. do. 15th January, 1820.
Rahn, John, lieutenant 16th	89.59	Do. do. 27th May, 1814, $14.59. He is since charged With $75 on account of contingencies; making this balance.
Rea, George, lieutenant 5th	500.00	Advanced on account of bounties and contingencies.
Robeson, Thomas I. major	7,722.15	Balance on settlement, 28th September, 1817. Reported for suit.
Ridgeway, Fielder, captain 1st riflemen	2,416.80	Do. do. 13th December, 1819, $1,416.90. Suspensions $687.32. He is also charged with $1,000 on account of Bounties, &c. Reported for suit.
Rind, William A. lieutenant, 36th	2,316.25	Advanced on account of bounties, &c. And reported for suit 15th March 1820.

STATEMENT--Continued

Names and Rank	Amount Dolls.Cts.	Remarks
Romayne, James T. B. captain	523.00	Balance on settlement, 27th November, 1817, $102. Suspensions $12. He is also charged with $421, on account of bounties and contingencies.
Roberts, Edward I. paymaster 1st infantry	5,564.73	Balance on settlement, 19th April, 1819.
Robinson, Nicholas, lieutenant 14th	193.75	Do. do. 25th February, 1819. Suspensions, 35.50.
Ritchie, John, captain artillery	1,453.40	Do. do. 3d December, 1819.

STATEMENT--Continued

Names and Rank	Amount Dolls.Cts.	Remarks
Ransom, Aaron, lieutenant	157.63	Balance on settlement, 27th June, 1818.
Rees, Joseph H. lieutenant and assist. dep. paymaster	330,729.22	Accounts and vouchers rendered, and apparent balance of $6,037.94.
Ropes, Benjamin, captain 21st	2,191.07	Balance on settlement, 21st July, 1819. Suspensions, $319.20.
Romayne, Samuel B. late 41st	32.00	Do. do. 1st December, 1817. Suspensions $32.
Reynolds, Abraham, dep. qr. Mas. Gen. N.Y. militia	11,220.47	Advanced on account of quartermaster department. Has rendered accounts and vouchers which require additional evidence that he has promised to supply.
Rathbone, William P. paymaster 32d	612.19	Balance on settlement, 4th August, 1820.
Rodney, C. A. paymaster volunteer artillery	156.36	Do. do. 28th February, 1818.
Ross, Edward, captain light dragoons	1,100.00	Account rendered, without vouchers, for $1,099.
Richardson, Thomas H. lieutenant 7th	1,526.00	Balance on settlement, 21st September, 1820. Reported for suit.
Ruffin, Robert R. lieutenant and paymaster artillery	54,418.20	Account and vouchers rendered, and apparent balance $11,625.66.
Rodes, Jason, paymaster volunteers	25,673.86	Balance on settlements, 3d November, 1820. Has further accounts to render.
Riley, B. ensign riflemen	143.34	Do. do. 9th November, 1818.
Roswell, Zachariah, captain 15th	2,450.00	Advanced on account of bounties, &c.
Rue, Benjamin S. lieutenant, 24th	58.92	Balance on settlement, 19th May, 1818.
Roberts, M. A. lieutenant 8th	278.00	Do. do. 17th August, 1818. Suspensions $8.
Randolph, Thomas B. lieutenant light artillery	150.00	Advanced on account of bounties, &c.
Rhodes, William, paymaster Kentucky militia	237.83	Balance on settlement, 19th April, 1820.
Rose, Charles R. lieutenant 35th	25.75	Do. do. 22d May, 1818. Suspensions $12.
Rico, Theodorick B. lieutenant 17th infantry	90.75	Balance on settlement, 25th May, 1818; arising from suspensions.
Rees, Jonathan, lieutenant, 7th	1,680.00	Advanced him on account of bounties, pay, and contingencies.
Respass, Robert C. paymaster 10th detach. Ken. Militia	13,969.19	Balance on settlement, 18th May, 1820. Reported for suit, 22d July, 1818.
Robinson, Simon, lieutenant, 30th	245.00	Advanced on account of bounties, &c.
Robb, Benjamin T. lieutenant artillery	2,310.00	Advanced on account of bounties, contingencies and quartermaster department.
Reed, John, Jun. lieutenant 9th	50.00	Advanced on account of bounties, &c.
Russell, Moses M. lieutenant artillery	814.00	Balance on settlement, 5th August, 1818. Suspensions $58.
Russell, John M. A. D. quartermaster general	6,424.27	Do. do. 18th August, 1818, and reported for suit 17th September, 1819.
Ryan, John H. lieutenant rifle regiment	200.00	Advanced on account of contingencies.
Rimington, Silas, surgeon	250.00	Advanced on account of medical and hospital department.
Rockwell, Samuel, lieutenant artillery	216.77	Balance on settlement, 22d September, 1818. Suspensions $32.

STATEMENT--Continued

Names and Rank	Amount Dolls.Cts.	Remarks
Robinson, William, Pennsylvania militia	14,287.54	Accounts on file and under examination.
Rogers, John D. lieutenant do.	40.00	Advanced on account of contingencies.
Randolph, Archibald C. captain	750.00	Advanced on account of bounties and contingencies.
Rogers, William, captain	910.48	Balance on settlement, 26th May, 1819. Suspensions $182.48. He has rendered additional accounts and vouchers $771.21. Apparent balance $139.27.

STATEMENT--Continued

Names and Rank	Amount Dolls.Cts.	Remarks
Robinson, John, ensign 12th	1,524.50	Advanced on account of bounties, contingencies and pay of the army.
Ruffin, John, lieutenant artillery	632.00	Balance on settlement, 8th December, 1819.
Rippey, Samuel A. lieutenant 22d	60.00	Do do 10th May, do
Rogers, John A. late A. D. quartermaster general	19,997.45	Do do 10th June, do Reported for suit 16th July, 1819.
Robinson, Henry, A. D. paymaster	7,407.57	Do do 30th December, do do do 7th January, 1820.
Read, George, to pay Delaware militia	3,171.74	Accounts rendered 5th December, 1817. This money was advanced to pay his company; it appears he has nearly completed the payments. This balance is due to individuals.
Robinson, Israel, to pay his company Virginia militia	586.52	Accounts rendered, and apparent balance due $81.75.
Ramsay, Thomas, captain 1st riflemen	334.60	Balance on settlement 24th July, 1815, $580.23. He has since refunded to P. M. general $245.63, leaving this balance. Has additional papers to file.
Richardson, Philip T. ensign 28th	800.00	Advanced on account of bounties, &c.
Roane, Fayette, lieutenant 2d dragoons	1,600.00	Advanced on account of bounties, &c. contingencies, pay of the army, and purchase of horses. Reported for suit 5th November, 1819.
Rudd, Richard, Kentucky militia	14,923.24	Accounts rendered, and under examination.
Rice, David B. paymaster	868.72	Balance on settlement, 7th July, 1820
Robinson, Jesse, 2d artillery	119.14	Do do 2d October, 1919 (1819) Suspensions $4.
Ray, William, late quartermaster 3d N. York militia	1,300.00	Do do 18th do Reported for suit 29th October, 1819.
Redmond, Henry H. lieutenant 36th	2,926.50	Do do 9th do Reported for suit 24th November, 1819.
Robinson, Hugh, lieutenant 13th	78.26	Do do 21st August, 1820. Suspensions, $52.54.
Staats, William B. ensign 6th	2,725.13	Do do 27th September, 1820. Has an account, without vouchers, for $2,838. Reported for suit, 30th September, 1820.
Stark, Jonathan, captain 11th	662.10	Do do 16th April, 1816. Suspensions, $573.11.
Scott, William G. lieutenant	111.63	Do Do 13th August, 1813, $11.63. Suspensions, $98. He is also charged with 100; making this balance.
Seward, Mason, lieutenant, 19th	92.00	Advanced on account of pay, bounties, and contingencies.
Stall, George W. lieutenant, 19th	638.09	Balance on settlement, 10th October, 1816. Suspensions, $362.
Simmons, John, ensign 19th	1,268.02	Do do 1st October, 1816, $318.02. He is also charged with $950; making this balance.
Scull, Jasper, Pennsylvania militia	19,626.04	Accounts rendered and under examination.
Scott, William T. lieutenant 3d riflemen	257.01	Balance on settlement, 24th November, 1815.

STATEMENT--Continued

Names and Rank	Amount Dolls.Cts.	Remarks
Staple, Elliott, lieutenant 34th	170.80	Account rendered, without vouchers, for $36.28.
Smith, Joseph D. lieutenant 34th	144.16	Balance on settlement, 1st February, 1814, $24.16. He is also charged with $120, on account of contingencies and bounties.
Sherman, lieutenant, 34th	1,170.00	Accounts rendered, without vouchers, for $222.77.
Shelton, William A. captain 20th	467.70	Balance on settlement, 23d June, 1820. Claims additional credits, not allowed for want of vouchers.
Scott, Edward H. lieutenant 36th	500.00	Advanced on account of bounties and contingencies.

STATEMENT--Continued

Names and Rank	Amount Dolls.Cts.	Remarks
Simmons, Asa W. ensign 11th	1,000.00	Advanced on account of bounties, &c.
Seeve, Ebenezer, lieutenant 33d	124.00	Balance on settlement, 11th February, 1820.
Staunton, P. brigade major volunteers	200.00	Advanced on account of pay of the army.
Simpson, Robert, doctor at St. Louis	77.03	Advanced on account of camp equipage, &c. It being a balance remaining in his hands as assistant military agent at Fort Madison, and brought to his debit on settlement of William Linnard's account.
Smith, John, lieutenant colonel 3d infantry	400.00	Advanced on account of bounties, &c, and camp equipage, &c.
Spencer, Thomas, lieutenant riflemen	60.43	Advanced on account of contingencies.
Seely, Robert G. lieutenant 2d infantry	48.39	Advanced on settlement, 7th June, 1813.
Sherman, Nathaniel, lieutenant, 6th	450.00	Advanced on account of bounties and contingencies.
Stetson, Amasa D. commissary	434.91	Advanced on account of camp equipage, &c.
Small, Francis W. lieutenant	411.17	Balance on settlement, 16th March, 1810.
Spann, John R. captain artillery	4. 7	do do 10th May, 1820
Shaw, Neal, lieutenant 6th	28.75	On account of contingencies for the transportation of his baggage from Albany to Pittsburg, the same being paid by Lieutenant Johnson, assistant agent at Fort Fayette, to which he was not entitled, supposed to be on furlough.
Scott, Charles, governor of Kentucky	2,500.00	Advanced on account of pay of rangers.
Suffers of the Connecticut Land Company	706.26	Advanced on account of Indian department. It being the amount paid by William Hull to certain Indians as part of said company's proportion of annuities for 1809 and 1810.
Smoot, John W. lieutenant 5th	72.69	Balance on settlement 19th June, 1815. Suspensions $8.
Saint, Daniel, lieutenant, 42d	699.75	Account rendered without vouchers, upon which he claims $275. He as received other moneys, leaving apparent balance of $624.50.
Sadlier, Clement, captain 6th	115.00	Advanced on account of quartermaster department.
Sevier, George W. lieutenant colonel	1,146.20	Balance on settlement 5th April, 1816.
Smith, Willis R. lieutenant 27th	300.00	Accounts rendered without vouchers, upon which he claims $180, apparent balance $120.
Shanks, Thomas W. ensign 21st	100.00	Advanced on account of bounties, &c. Has a claim for pay, &c.
Sturgess, William, lieutenant 22d	1,195.81	Balance on settlement, 17th May, 1814, $60.81. Suspensions $32. He is also charged with $1,135, making this balance.
Schener, Jacob, captain 16th	386.50	Accounts and vouchers rendered, upon which he claims $163.50; apparent balance, $386.50. Written to about this account.

STATEMENT--Continued

Names and Rank	Amount Dolls.Cts.	Remarks
Stockton, Samuel, ensign, 7th	132.63	Balance on settlement 29th April, 1820.
Sterry, Robert, Major and inspector general	193.69	Advanced on account of militia and quartermaster department.
Summer, Joseph, lieutenant 34th	300.00	Advanced on account of bounties, &c.
Sanderson, James P.	200.00	Advanced on account of contingencies.
Stockton, George, captain 28th	664.00	Advanced on account of bounties, &c.
Sill, David, quartermaster New York militia	123.00	Balance on settlement, 28th March, 1815.

STATEMENT--Continued

Names and Rank	Amount Dolls.Cts.	Remarks
Smith, Benjamin, lieutenant 2d	230.00	Advanced on account of quartermaster department and bounties, &c.
Seymour, Thomas S. ensign 25th	818.00	Advanced on account of bounties and contingencies.
Stanton, E. G. quartermaster militia	1,000.00	Advanced on account of quartermaster department and contingencies.
Shaw, Robert, captain, 42d	1,156.37	Balance on settlement, 31st December, 1819. Claims a balance for vouchers requiring explanation.
Sackrider, C. major militia	300.00	Advanced on account of militia.
Shotwell, William, captain 42d	3,088.00	Advanced on account of bounties, pay, and contingencies.
Smith, Nathaniel, lieutenant 39th	1,158.81	Balance on settlement 10th August, 1816. Suspensions of $525.25.
Stuart, Thomas, captain, 39th	2,380.00	Account rendered without vouchers, upon which he claims $264, leaving apparent balance, $2,116.
Spencer, Anderson, lieutenant 26th	259.00	Advanced on account of bounties &c.
Steward, John, ensign 32d	326.91	Account rendered, upon which he claims $208.50; apparent balance, $2,116.
Strong, Joseph C.	262.25	Advanced on account of medical and hospital department.
Spalding, Nathaniel, lieutenant 30th	378.26	Balance on settlement, 28th December, 1816. Suspensions $144.
Shackleford, Clement, captain Virginia militia	11.30	do do 31st August, 1820.
Smith, William W. lieutenant artillery	100.00	Advanced on account of medical and hospital department
Shea, Stephen, lieutenant 1st infantry	21.79	Balance on settlement, 24th October, 1816. Suspensions $23.30.
Stith, John W. Captain 34th	300.00	Advanced on account of bounties, &c.
Scofield, Joseph, lieutenant 15th	100.00	Account and vouchers rendered, upon which he claims $50, leaving an apparent balance of $50.
Stediford G. general	3,000.00	Advanced on account of contingencies. Accounted for by accounts for court martial expenses. Not yet settled by the office of the 2d Auditor.
Smith, Benjamin, lieutenant, 46th	350.00	Advanced on account of quartermaster department.
Schovel, Asahael, captain	50.00	do do do
Stull, John J. captain militia	50.00	do do do
Scott, Robert, captain 4th riflemen	40.13	Balance on settlement, 28th March 1816. Suspensions $51.74.
Snyder, Thomas, brigadier general Penn. Militia	10.00	Advanced on account of quartermaster department.
Stoor, Israel, lieutenant, 37th	30.00	Advanced on account of bounties, &c.
Steele, Matthew S. ensign	10.00	Advanced on account of quartermaster department.
Shannon, James, ensign 19th	300.00	Advanced on account of bounties, &c.
Shane, Abraham, lieutenant, 27th	127.84	Balance on settlement, 8th May, 1820.
Spencer, John, captain, 27th	60.00	Advanced on account of contingencies.

STATEMENT--Continued

Names and Rank	Amount Dolls.Cts.	Remarks
Spafford, Amos	2,650.89	Advanced on account of the quartermaster department, for the claims of sundry persons in Ohio, for corn taken and used by order of the general officers of the north western army in 1813, for which he is held accountable to produce the receipts of the individuals.
Sanborn, Matthew N. captain, 40th	23.66	Balance on settlement, 8th November, 1816.
Smith, Daniel, lieutenant 29th	361.09	Do do 16th August, 1816. Suspensions $362.14
Salisbury, Reuben, lieutenant 30th	118.00	Advanced on account of bounties and contingencies.

STATEMENT--Continued

Names and Rank	Amount Dolls.Cts.	Remarks
Smith, David, lieutenant	345.73	Balance n settlement, 13th May, 1820.
Stith, Drury, ensign	891.00	Do do 1st October, 1816. Suspensions, $854.97.
Sparks, Richard, colonel	10,290.80	Do do 27th September, 1820, and reported for suit 9th November, 1820
Scott, Daniel L. quartermaster	239.01	Do. do 27th November, 1817. Suspensions.
Swartwout, Robert, quartermaster general	137.92	Do do 10th April, 1817, $37.92
Simons, Rololphus, lieutenant, 23d	50.56	Do do 5th January, 1819. Suspensions, $39.50.
Scammon, George, lieutenant	35.61	Do do 3d October, 1818. Suspensions $42.56.
Scruggs Buford, lieutenant, 7th	287.24	Do do 3d May, 1817; arising from suspensions.
Simple, John, lieutenant	15.00	Advanced on account of quartermaster department.
Strother, William, major 18th	1,883.72	Balance on settlement, 29th June, 1820. Suspensions $232, and reported for suit.
Strother, Benjamin, lieutenant 2d riflemen	1,150.00	Advanced on account of bounties and contingencies
Scott, William, lieutenant 2d	378.94	Balance on settlement, 22d April, 1819. Suspensions $19, and reported for suit, 26th September, 1820.
Springer, Edward, lieutenant 34th	321.94	Do do 20th May, 1817, $382. He has since received a credit leaving this balance.
Sands, A. L. lieutenant artillery	1,204.43	Do do 14th April, 1819
Sturgis, Minor, lieutenant 34th	1,100.00	Account rendered without vouchers for $173.37.
Saunders, Benjamin W. captain 17th	1,645.00	Advanced on account of bounties, pay, and contingencies.
Sheldon, Walter, deputy paymaster	9,303.55	Balance on settlement, 2d May, 1820, and reported for suit same day.
Scott, Luther, lieutenant artillery	926.76	Do do 24th March, 1818. Suspensions, $595.05.
Smith, William lieutenant 18th	2,194.00	Do do 8th June, 1817, and reported for suit 20th September, 1819. Suspensions $210.
Smith, Samuel lieutenant 18th	1,210.00	Do do 5th June, 1817. Suspensions $84.50, and reported for suit, 14th December, 1819.
Street, John, lieutenant 18th infantry	291.95	Do do 3d January, 1820. Arising from suspensions.
Sparks, John B. lieutenant 14th	481.59	Do do 3d January, 1820. Suspensions $376.12.
Stark, Robert B. lieutenant	20.00	Advanced on account of contingencies.
Stephens, S. jun. paymaster 31st	630.82	Balance on settlement, 20th September, 1820.
Simons, Royal D. lieutenant 34th	709.00	Do do 17th July, 1817. Suspensions, $173.34.
Seldon, Martin L. lieutenant 30th	344.41	Do do 8th August, 1817. Suspensions, $324.
Smith, Elisha, lieutenant, 30th	96.13	Do do 9th August, 1817.
Swoyer, Jacob, lieutenant, 5th	454.20	Do do 4th January, 1820. Arising from suspensions.

STATEMENT--Continued

Names and Rank	Amount Dolls.Cts.			Remarks
Stockton, Thomas, captain 42d	2,926.00	Do	do	4th January, 1820. Says he has vouchers to render.
Smurr, Elias, lieutenant 4th riflemen	231.51	Do	do	21st February, 1819.
Scott, David, captain 23d	345.73	Do	do	15th May, 1820. Suspensions $196.20, and reported for suit.
Smith, Richard C. adjutant and lieutenant, 13th	2,662.30	Do	do	29th December, 1819. Suspensions $117.50.
Sproull, John, captain 13th	558.32	Do	do	19th March, 1818.
Smith, Charles, lieutenant 44th	411.31	Do	do	5th February, 1819.
Shipp, Edmund, lieutenant riflemen	147.75	Do	do	3d September, 1817.

STATEMENT--Continued

Names and Rank	Amount Dolls.Cts.	Remarks
Shield, Josiah, ensign 11th	1,081.00	Balance on settlement, 28th December, 1819. Suspensions $175. Reported by Capt. Gordon to be dead.
Siger, Asa B. major 29th	1,398.80	Do do 10th September, 1817.
Steuart, Josephus B. paymaster	18,310.78	Do do 29th December, 1819.
Smith, Malancton, colonel	20,498.89	Do do 8th October, 1820. Reported for suit 9th November, 1820.
Spencer, A. P. captain 29th	5,768.80	Do do 27th July, 1819. Suspensions $262.08. Reported for suit, 17th November, 1819.
Smith, Harold, lieutenant 2d artillery	200.00	Advanced on account of bounties, &c.
Shomo, Joseph, lieutenant 12th	305.14	Balance on settlement, 29th November, 1819. Suspensions 106 dollars.
Stanley, Nathaniel, captain 45th	38.00	Do do 13th September, 1817. Suspensions 8 dollars.
Steuart, James M. lieutenant 22d	159.50	Do do 6th January, 1819. Suspensions $78.50.
Strong, Return, lieutenant, 30th	34.23	Do do 19th September, 1819. Suspensions $4.
Sproat, James W. ensign 16th	149.75	Do do 29th September, 1818. Suspensions $115.37.
Stephens, William, lieutenant 34th infantry	369.00	Balance on settlement 19th November, 1816, 224 dollars, arising from suspensions; he is also charged with 145 dollars, making this balance.
Sheldon, George B. lieutenant 4th riflemen	1,708.00	Advanced on account of bounties and contingencies.
Schuyler, Peter P. colonel	121.20	On account of subsistence, for this sum brought to his debt for double rations paid him as commanding the recruiting department, No. 5.
Spencer, Philip D. paymaster	24,658.31	Balance on settlement, 4th May, 1818; and reported for suit, 10th June, 1818.
Scott, Richard W. lieutenant 35th	825.00	Accounts rendered without vouchers for $922.52
Steuart, Charles, lieutenant 15th	1,858.00	Advanced on account of bounties, pay, and contingencies.
Smith, Charles, captain 2d dragoons	3,992.70	Balance on settlement, 3d December, 1819. Suspensions, $1,763.80.
Scott, Winfield, lieutenant colonel	5,517.92	Has accounts for expenditures made, to render, which, from his representation, will account for this balance.
Smith, Francis, ensign 2d infantry	268.00	Balance on settlement, 24th February, 1818, arising from suspensions.
Sisk, John, ensign 6th	2,910.00	Do. do. 6th January, 1820. Reported for suit, 27th September, 1820. Has rendered an account, without vouchers, for $168.44.
Stakle, Joseph, ensign 22d	158.00	Do. do. 14th February, 1820. Suspensions 8 dollars.
Smith, G D. captain 6th	121.59	Do. do. 27th April, 1818.

STATEMENT--Continued

Names and Rank	Amount Dolls.Cts.	Remarks
Symmes, John C. lieutenant 1st infantry	512.67	Do. do. 14th November, 1816, $62.67; he is also charged with 450 dollars, making this balance. He has rendered accounts for $426.25, of which $60.25 is vouched.
Smith, James, lieutenant 30th	340.00	Advanced on account of bounties, &c.
Staniford, Thomas, paymaster 11th	16,703.72	Balance on settlement, 24th May, 1820. Petitioned Congress for lost vouchers; relief not granted. Reported for suit.
Sutphur, Aaron, captain 15th	2,540.24	Do. do. 31st August, 1818, $110.24. Suspensions 216 dollars. He is also charged with 2,430 dollars.
Smith, Charles, lieutenant 16th	150.00	Advanced on account of bounties, pay, and contingencies.

Names and Rank	Amount Dolls.Cts.	Remarks
Shannon, William, lieutenant 3d artillery	940.00	Has rendered accounts, without vouchers, for $690.98.
Smalley, Daniel, lieutenant	449.37	Balance on settlement, 19th May, 1820. Suspensions $549.10.
Sangster, Thomas, captain 2d infantry	4,916.60	Do. do. 28th December, 1819. Says he will attend to settlement of his accounts.
Shang, William H. ensign 17th	1,870.00	Do. do. 19th May, 1819. Suspensions 403 dollars, and Reported for suit 9th Nov. 1820.
Swearengen, John, lieutenant 2d riflemen	318.00	Balance on settlement, 14th December, 1818. Suspensions 4 dollars.
Stockton, John, lieutenant 2d	595.75	Do. do. 5th February, 1819. Suspensions 8 dollars.
Steuart, Rufus, captain, 31st	3,252.00	Advanced on account of bounties and contingencies.
Smith, Phillips, lieutenant, 30th	366.00	Balance on settlement, 9th October, 1818. Suspensions 116 dollars.
Smith, Robert, lieutenant 19th	500.00	Advanced on account of bounties, &c.
Sparks, C. A. lieutenant 3d rflemen	40.00	Advanced on account of contingencies.
Senter, German, surgeon's mate 3d artillery	345.22	Advanced on account of medical and hospital department.
Smith, Richard, captain	500.00	Advanced on account of quartermaster department.
Starr, Henry, lieutenant and paymaster 37th	1,141.16	Balance on settlement, 15th January, 1820.
Strobel, Martin, paymaster South Carolina militia	5,000.00	Accounts and vouchers rendered, and reported for suit 22d July, 1818.
Sneed, Archibald H. deputy paymaster	421,260.48	Accounts and vouchers rendered, and in the course of adjustment. He has additional accounts to render.
Sharer, Philip S. ensign 27th	300.00	Advanced on account of bounties and contingencies.
Steele, George G	1,748.20	States that all his paper were lost at the battle of Stoney Creek, where He was captured.
Simons, Peter, ensign 43d	198.98	Balance on settlement, 7th August, 1818. Suspensions $72.35.
Seaman, Gilbert, captain, 41st	369.87	Do. do. 12th do. Suspensions 8 dollars.
Spencer, Gideon, lieutenant, 26th	31.43	Do. do. 28th December, 1819. Suspensions 12 dollars.
Stallings, Elias, captain 1st riflemen	470.34	Do. do. 3d September, 1818. Suspensions $99.31.
Shubrick, Thomas, lieutenant	100.00	Advanced on account of bounties, &c.
Snelling, Josiah, colonel	763.60	Balance on settlement, 4th September, 1818. Suspensions $40.70.
Sprogle, Thomas Y. lieutenant 22d, deceased	1,474.19	Do. do. 6th October, 1818. Suspensions $940.44, and reported for suit 14th December, 1819.
Simpson, Joseph S. ensign 14th	501.00	Do. do. 5th October, 1818. Reported for suit, 26th September, 1820.
Strother, John, lieutenant, 12th	14.46	Do. do. 23d October, 1818. Suspensions 12 dollars.
Shannon, Samuel, late paymaster 27th	3,450.46	Do. do. 24th January, 1820
Stephens, Thomas, lieutenant, 30th	68.98	Do. do. 9th October, 1818. Suspensions 30 dollars.

STATEMENT--Continued

Names and Rank	Amount Dolls.Cts.	Remarks
Swearengen, Henry V. lieutenant riflemen	3,678.05	Do. do. 17th September, 1819; and reported for suit 20th September, 1819.
Scott, Benjamin H. lieutenant 9th	179.25	Do. do. 12 March, 1819. Suspensions $20.30
Sullivan, Clement, captain 14th infantry	44.38	Balance on settlement, 8th February, 1819. Suspensions $45.08.
Sweet, William, captain 14th infantry	764.74	Do do. 17th May, 1820. Suspensions $26.40.
Smith, Guy, lieutenant 39th	9,055.31	Accounts and vouchers rendered for $159.25. He states that the sum of $8,536.24 is for provisions turned over to him, which he regularly issued to the 39th regiment; and that $350.07 is for a bill of exchange drawn by him on the Secretary of War.

STATEMENT--Continued

Names and Rank	Amount Dolls.Cts.	Remarks
Sheffey, Daniel, act.paymaster to sundry Vir. Militia	705.26	Balance on settlement, 21st April, 1820.
Smith, Josiah A. late paymaster Maryland militia	123.90	Do do 26th March, 1819.
Schener, Jacob, captain, 16th infantry	999.38	Do do 28th March, 1820.
Smith, Jasper Y. paymaster riflemen	428.83	Do do 12th April, 1819.
Stannard, John, lieutenant colonel	120.00	Advanced on account of bounties, &c.
Stewart, Alexander, major	900.00	Balance on settlement, 12th April 1819.
Stokes, John R. captain 2d dragoons	1,510.00	Accounts rendered for $1,261.05; vouchers only for $890.05; leaving apparent balance of $248.95.
Scott, Chasteen, lieutenant 17th	361.25	Balance on settlement, 29th March, 1820. Suspensions $238.50, and has a claim for pay, &c.
Scholtz, John G. lieutenant 27th	5,592.96	Do do 29th April, 1819. Suspensions $492.37.
Saunders, Lewis	20,000.00	Advanced him by an order of the commanding general, to pay arrearages of rations to Militia. No account or vouchers rendered. Reported for suit, 17th May, 1819.
Sutherland, Solomon, captain 29th	144.34	Balance on settlement, 29th May, 1819. Suspensions $92.02.
Smith, William, lieutenant 2d artillery	972.00	Advanced on account of bounties, pay, and contingencies.
Sampson, John, quartermaster New York militia	135.68	Balance on settlement, 13th July, 1819.
Smith, James, paymaster 1st Ohio militia	7,506.11	Do do 16th June, 1820. Reported for suit.
Smith, John H. paymaster Ohio militia	7,951.55	Do do 30th July, 1819, and reported for suit, 14th October, 1819.
Smith, Thomas T. lieutenant 1st riflemen	300.00	Advanced on account of quartermaster department.
State of Rhode Island	31,917.62	Advanced on account of pay, subsistence, and forage.
Sneed, Junius D. paymaster	124,478.31	Accounts and vouchers rendered, and apparent balance refunded.
Swift, John, assistant deputy paymaster	11,498.45	Balance on settlement, 19th May, 1820.
Smith, Thomas L. paymaster 5th N. Carolina militia	1,275.92	Do do 30th August, 1819. Reported for suit 3d October, 1820.
Stevens, James, South Carolina militia	610.27	Accounts on file and under examination.
Searcey, Robert, acting paymaster	802,801.96	Accounts and vouchers rendered and apparent balance $31,874.66, which he has been called upon to return. He is now dead, and his accounts, which are very voluminous are preparing for suit.
Shewell, Nathaniel, paymaster Pennsylvania militia	445.56	Balance on settlement, 15th May, 1820.
Stephenson, B. to pay Illinois militia	8,123.81	Vouchers rendered, but no account current. Appears to have disbursed the amount charged.

STATEMENT--Continued

Names and Rank	Amount Dolls.Cts.	Remarks
Shaumburg, Bartholomew, assistant D. paymaster	155,000.00	Accounts and vouchers rendered and under examination.
Shoemaker, Rudolph I. assist. paymaster N.Y. militia	19,000.00	Advanced on account of pay, subsistence and forage.
Smyth, William captain 1st riflemen	4,740.49	Balance on settlement, 22d October, 1819. Suspensions $180.93.
Smyth, Augustus C. lieutenant colonel 12th	2,270.00	Do do 22 June, 1815, $130.55. He is also charged with other moneys, making this balance.
Strother, George, captain, 10th	16.75	Balance on settlement, 22d June, 1815, $550.70. He has since refunded to the paymaster general $535.95; leaving this balance.
Shell, Henry, lieutenant 6th	16.00	Advanced on account of pay of the army.
Saunders, William G. lieutenant 14th	10.00	Advanced on account of pay of the army.

STATEMENT--Continued

Names and Rank	Amount Dolls.Cts.	Remarks
Scott, Samuel, 24th reg.	33,134.40	Accounts rendered and under examination.
Strode, Thomas, captain 5th infantry	900.28	Balance on settlement, 4th January, 1820.
Shaylor, Ephraham ensign	18.00	Advanced on account of bounties, &c.
Sanford, Daniel, Virginia militia	55,783.80	Accounts on file and under examination.
Swift, Joseph G. brigadier general	1,000.00	Advanced on account of quartermaster department.
Schuyler, Barent, captain 29th	5,492.84	Balance on settlement, 24th August, 1816, $4,672.84. Suspensions $219. He is also charged with $20, making this balance.
Snead, Benjamin, captain 11th	278.38	Balance on settlement, 16th October, 1819.
Steele, Robert, captain	1,500.00	Advanced on account of quartermaster department.
Simmons, William late accountant of war	1,779.93	Balance on settlement, 31st March, 1812; and reported for suit 16th November, 1819.
Stockton, Robert, lieutenant 19th	550.00	Do do 12th July, 1816, $530. Suspensions $219. He is also charged with $20; making this balance.
Simkins, Arthur, captain	724.21	Balance on settlement, 23d June, 1814. $603.71. He is also charged with other moneys; making this balance.
Stewart, Timothy, paymaster 2d New York militia	1,168.90	Balance on settlement, 4th December, 1819.
Skinner, David, paymaster New York militia	3,041.32	Do do 21st December, 1819.
Schoonmaker, Zachariah, paymaster New York volunteers	5,454.28	Do do 17th March, 1820. Suspensions $181.43; and reported for suit 28th October, 1820.
Smith, Philip, lieutenant, 26th	107.60	Do do August, 1818. Suspensions $106.20.
Tyler, William, lieutenant	155.00	Accounts and vouchers rendered, upon which he claims a balance.
Tyler, Edmund, Virginia militia	48,788.92	Accounts on file, and under examination.
Taylor, James D. paymaster	18,716.75	Accounts reported by the 3d Auditor, exhibiting this balance on the ---May, 1820; not yet acted upon. He claims credits to the amount of the balance, which have not been allowed by the Auditor.
Tennelle, William A. agent for paying claims	6,785.90	Balance on settlement, 3d August, 1820. Reported for suit, 10th November, 1820.
Thomas, George W. ensign 34th	60.00	Advanced on account of bounties and contingencies.
Taylor, Richard, deputy quartermaster general	12,000.00	Advanced on account of quartermaster department, for supplies to Kentucky militia. Has promised to render his accounts.
Todd, Robert, lieutenant	100.00	Advanced on account of quartermaster department.
Templeman, George, lieutenant 26th	952.40	Balance on settlement, 28th July, 1815.
Thompson, Joseph, captain, 28th	231.15	Do do 17th February, 1817. Suspensions 75 dollars.

STATEMENT--Continued

Names and Rank	Amount Dolls.Cts.	Remarks
Townsend, Solomon D. late captain	33.00	On account of subsistence, for amount received from James S. Swearengen, for double rations as commanding Bedlow's Island in 1809, to which he was not entitled.
Tannehill, Adamson, brigadier general	500.00	Advanced on account of militia.
Taite, J. C. lieutenant, 39th	50.00	Advanced on account of contingencies.
Trumbo, John, lieutenant, 28th	150.00	Advanced on account of bounties, &c.
Terry, Noah, captain sea fencibles	200.00	Advanced on account of contingencies.

Names and Rank	Amount Dolls.Cts.	Remarks
Taylor, Ebenezer, captain volunteer cavalry	200.00	Advanced on account of contingencies.
Talliaferro, M. captain, 35th	20.00	Advanced on account of contingencies.
Townsley, William, lieutenant riflemen	51.62	Balance on settlement, 23d March, 1820.
Talbott, R. C. captain, 26th	867.75	Do do 1st January, 1817. Suspensions $742.25.
Trotter, George, colonel Kentucky militia	370.00	Advanced on account of quartermaster department.
Tepton, Jacob, ensign riflemen	96.00	Balance on settlement May, 1820.
Timberlake, William M. lieutenant 43d	174.61	Balance on settlement, 4th October, and 12th Decmeber, 1816. $74. He is also charged with $100.
Turner, Tilman, ensign 3d	600.00	Balance on settlement, 21 September, 1820.
Tracey, David, lieutenant 37th	104.00	Advanced on account of bounties, &c.
Thompson, Festus L. lieutenant 26th	361.25	Balance on settlement, 22d May, 1816, $23.50. Suspensions $237.76. He is also charged with $325.75.
Taylor, Nathaniel, brigadier general	500.00	Advanced on account of quartermaster department.
Tieman, Peter, quartermaster Mississippi dragoons	100.00	Advanced on account of quartermaster department.
Tatham, William	100.00	Advanced on account of contingencies.
Thompson, Ephraim, ensign 24th	132.00	Advanced on account of bounties, &c.
Trigg, William major 28th	30.84	Advanced on account of contingencies.
Taylor, Samuel A. lieutenant 43d	45.38	Balance on settlement, 12th February, 1820. Suspensions $75.
Tatnal, Edward F. lieutenant 43d	58.93	Do do 6th April, 1818.
Tyler, John, lieutenant, 25th	25.00	Do do 28th March, 1817. Suspensions $88.17.
Taylor, Henry P. captain, 18th	1,496.42	Do do 30th October, 1819. Reported for suit 10th November, 1819.
Talmage, C. B. paymaster	2092.61	Do do 23d August, 1819.
Tompkins, Daniel D. late governor of New York	4,411.25	An advance made by the Secretary of War, for being the lost on the sale of Treasury notes, which requires legislative sanction.
Tompkins, Daniel D. late governor of New York	11,022.57	Balance on his account settled 14th June, 1820.
Truax, John B. ensign 33d	1,583.32	Balance on settlement 28th November, 1818. Suspensions $20. Reported for suit 26th September, 1820. Has additional Accounts for $310, without vouchers.
Tracey, J. L. lieutenant	36.00	Balance on settlement, 3d July, 1818
Tuttle, John L. lieutenant colonel	3,157.97	Do do 4th November, 1819, and reported for suit 10th November, 1819.
Talbott, Josiah G. lieutenant 26th	148.50	Do do 9th January 1818.
Thornton, A. W. captain artillery	4,406.17	Do do 9th November, 1819. Reported for suit 18th December, 1819.

STATEMENT--Continued

Names and Rank	Amount Dolls.Cts.	Remarks
Ten Eyck, Abraham, captain	762.95	Do do 20th January, 1818.
Tappan, Samuel, ensign 23d	151.48	Do do 29th May, 1815, $28.40. Suspensions 52 dollars. He is also charged with $123.
Turner, Thomas, ensign	124.00	Do do 27th April, 1820. Arising from suspensions.
Tupper, Edward, Ohio militia	1,746.76	Accounts rendered, which require explanation and further vouchers.
Thomas, John, major general militia	903.60	Balance on settlement, 5th February, 1818.
Thayer, Sylvanus	134.00	Do do 26th June, 1813, 4 dollars. He is since charged with 130 dollars; making this balance.

STATEMENT--Continued

Names and Rank	Amount Dolls.Cts.	Remarks
Thompson, Francis, paymaster 43d Md. Militia	23.78	Balance on settlement, 20th April, 1818.
Tarrant, John, lieutenant	600.00	Accounts rendered without vouchers for $43.60.
Thompson, John W. lieutenant 14th infantry	50.00	Balance on settlement, 1st June, 1818.
Todd, George W. colonel 17th	5,591.00	Do. do. 25th September, 1819. Suspensions $124.50. Reported for suit 27th September, 1819.
Taylor, John, lieutenant 17th	1,200.00	Advanced on account of bounty, pay, and contingencies.
Toby, Charles, captain 21st	450.00	Accounts rendered for 658 dollars, without vouchers.
Taylor, Bushrod, paymaster Virginia militia	5,121.19	Balance on settlement, 7th March, 1819.
Taylor, James, captain 30th	64.18	Do. do. 12th June, 1818. Suspensions 98 dollars.
Thompson, John L. lieutenant 43d	184.55	Do. do. 23d June, 1818, arising from suspensions.
Turner, Samuel D. paymaster	102,477.52	Do. do. 19th June, 1820. Has additional claims on vouchers suspended, further evidence required.
Thompson, Ebenezer, captain, 9th	659.37	Do. do. 11th May, 1819. Suspensions $176.85; and reported for suit 26th September, 1820.
Townsend, Isaac, lieutenant 34th	178.00	Do. do. 29th July, 1818. Suspensions, $19.77.
Turpin, Beverly, lieutenant 2d dragoons	876.56	Do. do. 4th August, 1818. Suspensions $564.62.
Trippe, James, lieutenant 2d dragoons	720.00	Accounts rendered without vouchers for 27 dollars.
Taylor, Charles N. lieutenant 38th	50.80	Balance on settlement, 2d July, 1819.
Turner, Israel, captain 13th	176.07	Do. do. 19th August, 1820. Suspensions 68 dollars.
Tate, Jesse O. lieutenant 39th	8.00	Do. do. 22d March, 1819.
Thompson, William, paymaster 36th Virginia militia	1,386.43	Do. do. 29th April, 1819.
Tuckerman, Benjamin, captain	16.38	Do. do. 9th June, 1819, arising from suspensions.
Thompson, William P. paymaster 5th Virginia militia	5,284.25	Do. do. 5th August, 1820. Reported for suit.
Torrance, Robert, quartermaster N. Carolina militia	1,620.00	Accounts rendered without vouchers for $458.31.
Turner, Samuel, lieutenant 10th	460.00	Advanced on account of bounties, pay and contingencies.
Ten Broeck, George W. captain 6th	7,259.96	Balance on settlement, 11th December, 1819, arising from suspensions. Reported for suit 27th Sept. 1820.
Tufts, Thomas, New York militia	4,902.72	Accounts on file and under examination.
Triplett, William, lieutenant 3d infantry	1,027.00	Balance on settlement, 8th December, 1819, and reported for suit 28th February, 1820.
Taylor, William, captain	200.00	No accounts rendered.
Thomas, Eli, lieutenant	50.00	No accounts or vouchers.
Terris, William B. lieutenant 30th	76.00	Advanced on account of bounties, &c.
Upham, Edward, lieutenant 3d infantry	1,010.00	Advanced on account of bounties and contingencies.
Vallean, John, lieutenant 13th	125.25	Balance on settlement, 14th July, 1813.

Names and Rank	Amount Dolls.Cts.	Remarks
Vosbury, Peter J. lieutenant colonel 9th infantry	650.00	Advanced on account of quartermaster department.
Vischer, N. J. captain riflemen	161.51	Balance on settlement, 16th November, 1811.
Vose, Josiah H. captain 9th	1,163.77	Do. do. 10th March, 1820. Reported for suit 17th September, 1819.
Vandergee, Storm T. wagonmaster	135.14	Do. do. 15th do. 1814.

STATEMENT--Continued

Names and Rank	Amount Dolls.Cts.	Remarks
Vance, Joseph, captain Ohio militia	269.27	Accounts on file, and under examination.
Vanderslice, Joseph H. lieutenant 22d	20.79	On account of pay and subsistence, it being an improper payment, made by Washington Lee, in 1813.
Vanderheyden, David, lieutenant	2,182.00	Balance on settlement, 12th November, 1819, and reported for suit 24th November, 1819.
Vance, Oliver, lieutenant 27th	298.14	Do. do. 17th July, 1817. arising from suspensions.
Voorhies, Peter G. D. paymaster	370,087.06	Accounts rendered and under examination. By his own statement, a balance of $25,378.11 appears to be due to the United States, which he has been required to return preparatory to the examination of his accounts.
Van Schaick, Garret H. paymaster	267.11	Balance on settlement 18th May, 1820. Suspensions $100.50.
Van Horne, Thomas B. lieutenant colonel 19th	425.62	Advanced on account of bounties and contingencies.
Vail, Samuel, captain 7th	1,088.00	Balance on settlement, 18th July, 1818. Suspensions 30 dollars.
Van Antwerp, Henry, lieutenant	829.78	do. do. 3d February, 1819. Suspensions $20.
Varnum, Jacob B. captain 40th	372.00	do. do. 15th January, 1819. Suspensions $112.
Van Buren, Lawrence quartermaster general	3,782.50	Advanced on account of militia.
Van Buren, P. B. captain 29th	1,450.34	Balance on settlement 27th June, 1816, $400.34; he is also charged with 1,050 dollars.
Van Vechten, Derrick C. paymaster	14.30	Do. do. 13th July, 1820, arising from suspensions.
Vail, Thomas, late ensign 29th	1,755.00	Do. do. 11th November, 1819. Reported for suit 24th November, 1819.
Vail, John, captain 18th	57.37	Do. do. 20th December, 1819, arising from suspensions.
Ward, James, commissary general	13,000.00	Advanced on account of subsistence and quartermaster department.
Willis, Perrin, lieutenant 2d artillery	3,579.75	Account rendered for pay, and states he has further accounts to render.
Walch, Michael, captain artillery	692.00	Balance on settlement, 10th January, 1820.
Warner, Henry W. paymaster New York militia	110.40	Do. do. 2nd March, 1820. Suspensions $17.74.
Warren, Joseph, quartermaster Ohio militia	100.00	Advanced on account of militia.
Wilson, Nathaniel, surgeon	100.00	Advanced on account of medical and hospital department.
Wilcox, David B. lieutenant 13th	743.67	Balance on settlement 13th December, 1813, $193.67. He is also charged with $550, making this balance.
West, I. assistant apothecary general	300.00	Advanced on account of medical and hospital department.
Wade, William, A. D. C. ordnance	150.00	Advanced on account of contingencies.
Wall, Joseph G. lieutenant 10th	544.00	Advanced on account of bounties and contingencies, and reported for Suit 26th September, 1820.

STATEMENT--Continued

Names and Rank	Amount Dolls.Cts.	Remarks
Woolsey, Melancton, A. D. quartermaster	27,844.36	Balance on settlement 31st August, 1820. Has further accounts to render, which his representative (he being dead) has promised to furnish.
Wilkinson, James B. captain 2d infantry	120.00	Balance on settlement, 11th January, 1820.
White, Ebenezer, captain 21st	370.00	Accounts rendered without vouchers, upon which he claims $641. He has received other moneys not yet at his debit, making an apparent balance of $48.20
Wade, Nathan C. ensign 10th	254.00	Accounts rendered, upon which he claims $24, without vouchers; balance, $230.
Wyche, George, lieutenant	202.00	Accounts rendered, without vouchers, upon which he claims $170.22. He has received other moneys, not yet to his debit, making the balance of $91.75.

STATEMENT--Continued

Names and Rank	Amount Dolls.Cts.	Remarks
Woodman, Benjamin, lieutenant 34th	312.59	Accounts rendered, upon which he claims $158.90.
Wickliff, M. H. Kentucky militia	18,931.28	Accounts on file, and under examination.
Wilkinson, William L. ensign 36th	95.00	Balance on settlement 10th December, 1813. He is also charged with $50 on account of bounties, &c.
White, Benedict, lieutenant 36th	110.50	Advanced on account of bounties and contingencies.
Williams, Barnett, paymaster Kentucky militia	9,913.02	Accounts and vouchers rendered, and apparent balance $619.18.
Ward, James, lieutenant 38th	30.00	Advanced on account of contingencies.
White, Samuel, captain volunteers	80.00	Advanced on account of pay of the army.
Wilson, Ebenezer, major volunteers	100.00	Advanced on account of pay of the army.
Wilcox, A. quartermaster militia	80.00	Advanced on account of pay of the army.
Wentzel, Alexander	40.00	Balance on settlement, 1st August, 1810.
Wadsworth, Elijah, major general	12,981.50	Advanced on account of militia and volunteers. Accounts and vouchers rendered, but so informal as not to be admissible, though the money has been expended.
Williams, Johnathan, col.	650.00	Advanced on account of completing fortifications. Vouchers on file, irregular and not deemed admissible.
White, Hays G. quartermaster	223.55	Accounts and vouchers rendered, upon which he claims $98, leaving an apparent balance of $1125.55.
Wallace, John C.	80.00	Advanced on account of militia.
Walton, John, & Co. at Schenectady, New York	500.00	On Account of quartermaster department. It being the amount paid by them by H. Glenn, A. D. quartermaster general, to reimburse them so much stated to have been advanced by them to boatmen that went as pilots in the boats to Oswego, but of which advance no evidence is produced.
Watts, Beauford T. A. D. quartermaster	2,500.00	Accounts and vouchers rendered, and apparent balance $946.90.
Walker, William, captain 25th	565.30	Balance on settlement, 21 January, 1820. Suspensions $60.
Warren, William lieutenant 19th	205.62	Do do 25th November, 1813, $180.62. He is also charged with $25, on account of contingencies, making this balance.
Weegy, Samuel, lieutenant 16th	34.18	Balance on settlement, 17th April, 1816.
Wenn, Thomas, lieutenant artillery	590.00	Do do 9th August, 1820. Reported for suit 26th September, 1820.
Williams, Eleazer	440.40	Advanced on account of quartermaster department.
Williams, Simon C. lieutenant 35th	196.00	Advanced on account of contingencies and bounties, &c.
Watson, R. lieutenant 25th	220.00	Advanced on account of bounties, &c.

STATEMENT--Continued

Names and Rank	Amount Dolls.Cts.	Remarks
Williams, I. lieutenant colonel militia	200.00	Advanced on account of bounties.
Whatley, Wilson, ensign 18th	850.00	Written to on the 16th December, 1819, and required to pay this balance.
Witherbee, Samuel, ensign, 31st	280.00	Accounts and vouchers rendered, upon which he claims $127.15. He has received other moneys, not yet to his debit, making an apparent balance $552.85
Willard, John S. lieutenant 31st	250.00	Advanced on account of contingencies.
Walker, Enos, lieutenant 31st	135.00	Balance on settlement, 22d September, 1820.
Ward, Uriah, captain, 31st	5.06	Do do 27th June, 1814.
Woods, Richard M. ensign 24th	82.24	Do do 26th May, 1816.

STATEMENT--Continued

Names and Rank	Amount Dolls.Cts.	Remarks
Wells, William S. ensign 17th	612.00	Advanced on account of bounties and contingencies, and reported for suit 26th September, 1820.
Wilson, John, lieutenant 32d	11.28	Balance on settlement 29th June, 1816.
Walker, P. P. assistant inspector general, Kentucky	60.00	Advanced on account of quartermaster department.
Westover, Ira, ensign 4th	50.00	Advanced on account of bounties, &c.
Williams, John, New York Militia	40.00	Advanced on account of contingencies.
Wheelock, Linneas	500.00	Advanced on account of quartermaster department.
Watson, John, captain militia cavalry	30.00	Advanced on account of quartermaster department.
Wilson, Andrew, captain	29.49	Balance on settlement, 25th September, 1815.
Womack, Jesse, lieutenant	126.00	Do do 23d February, 1820.
Watts, George, lieutenant dragoons	30.00	Advanced on account of pay of the army.
Ward, Charles, ensign 26th	95.00	Balance on settlement, 24th October, 1820.
Whitsett, William, Kentucky militia	30,882.62	Accounts rendered and under examination.
Weed, Harvey, paymaster New York militia	73.16	Balance on settlement, 21st February, 1820. Suspensions $8.
Will, George, ensign 26th	167.06	Do do 10th June, 1816.
Williams, D. D. secretary S. C. com's on fortifications	2,968.87	Advanced on account of fortifications.
Whittelsey, Samuel, paymaster New York militia	4,113.54	Balance on settlement, 1st October, 1816.
Wadham, Heman, lieutenant 30th	495.00	Advanced on account of bounties, &c.
Weeks, Scherick, lieutenant 30th	236.00	Advanced on account of bounties, &c.
Watts, James R., lieutenant 23d	31.93	Balance on settlement, 27th May, 1816.
Wooding, J. C. ensign 1st infantry	300.00	Advanced on account of bounties, pay, and contingencies.
Walker, William, sub agent	608.24	On account of subsistence, for subdry provisions turned over to him.
Worth, William J. captain 23d	32.20	Balance on settlement, 29th October, 1819.
Walker, William, captain 39th	198.34	Do do 7th April, 1817, $128.34. Suspensions $74. He is also charged with $170 on account of bounties and credited with $100; leaving this balance.
Wood, Eleazer, colonel	80.00	Advanced him on account of bounties, &c.
Walker, James, lieutenant 33d	120.20	Balance on settlement, 30th March, 1819.
Winston, William O.	461.76	Do do 30th December, 1815, and 1st January, 1816, $1155.14. He has since received credit for $693.38; leaving this balance.
Watson, Benjamin, major	1,073.70	Do do 24th September, 1817. Suspensions $8.
Wayne, William C. lieutenant 8th	1,200.00	Reported for suit 5th November, 1819.
Wyatt, John, lieutenant 28th	250.00	Advanced on account of bounties and contingencies.

STATEMENT--Continued

Names and Rank	Amount Dolls.Cts.	Remarks
Wheelock, P. lieutenant 4th	4.00	Balance on settlement 9th October, 1818, $280.28. Suspensions $4. He has since refunded to the paymaster general $276.28; leaving this balance.
Williams, John, lieutenant, 13th	388.42	Do do 1st September, 1820.
Wilde James, lieutenant 8th infantry	984.67	Do do 18th May, 1818.

Names and Rank	Amount Dolls.Cts.	Remarks
Winder, William H. lieutenant colonel	4,484.85	Balance on settlement, 22d March, 1820.
White, Philip, captain 9th	427.10	Do do 9th March, 1818. Suspensions $626.05.
Wiley, James, lieutenant 33d	91.66	Do do 4th May, 1818. Suspensions $107.35.
Wellborne, James, colonel	543.60	Advanced on account of bounties, and pay of the army.
Welch, William, lieutenant 43d	74.10	Balance on settlement 5th August, 1817. Suspensions $24.
Whitlock, E. L. major 15th	16.00	Advanced on account of bounties, &c.
Way, Ebenezer, captain	981.90	Balance on settlement 24th October, 1818.
Wells, James, lieutenant 11th	186.41	Do do 11th November, 1818. Suspensions $154.
Waterman, F. Y. captain 29th	59.59	Do do 16th September, 1818. Suspensions $50.37.
Watkins, John, captain volunteers	9.75	Do do 11th December, 1817.
Woodward, Francis, lieutenant 24th	2,876.00	Do do 28th September, 1817. Suspensions $124.
Whiting, Henry, lieutenant 23d	170.28	Do do 4th November, 1819.
Webster, Nathaniel, ensign 33d	505.66	Do do 24th September, 1818. Suspensions $327.35.
Wager, Philip, lieutenant and quartermaster 4th infantry	52.08	Do do 24th March, 1819.
Wilcox, Delafayette, lieutenant 25th	328.73	Do do 9th January, 1818; written to 16th December, 1819, and required to bay this balance. Reported for suit 26th September, 1820.
Wilcocks, J. major volunteer cavalry	2,245.20	Will be accounted for on settlement of the account of the Canadian corps.
Weston, Samuel, paymaster volunteers	2,580.20	Balance on settlement 7th February, 1820. Suspensions $946.50
Wildey, Joshua, captain 23d	464.96	Do do 11th January, 1819. Suspensions $230.85.
Weitzell, George, paymaster Pennsylvania militia	2,193.33	Do do 30th March, 1819. Reported for suit 3d October, 1820.
Warner, George, paymaster 51st Pennsylvania militia	548.03	Do do 10th April, 1819. Suspensions $304.32.
Wyncoop, John , ensign 34th	26.00	Do do 5th March, 1819.
White, Edward, lieutenant 7th	747.00	Do do 21st September, 1820, and reported for suit 30th September, 1820.
Weaver, John, lieutenant, 7th	1,084.00	Advanced on account of bounties, pay and contingencies.
Welton, Philo, late paymaster New York militia	361.11	Balance on settlement 11th April, 1818. Suspensions $105.77.
Willis, Lewis B. captain	7,305.90	Written to on the subject of his account 2d December, 1819; required to account for this balance.
Wingate, Thomas S. quartermaster Kentucky militia	800.00	This money will be accounted for on settlement of Willis Floyd's accounts.
Wright, Benjamin, captain 39th	555.64	Balance on settlement 1st April, 1818. Suspensions $199.03.

STATEMENT--Continued

Names and Rank	Amount Dolls.Cts.	Remarks
Wilkinson, James, major general	5,557.63	Do do 11th October, 1819, $5,457.63. He is since charged with 100 dollars; making this balance.
Walters, Francis, lieutenant 15th	500.00	Advanced on account of bounties and contingencies.
Wallace, Benjamin, major	6,098.26	Balance on settlement, 10th July, 1818. Suspensions $202.71, and reported for suit 17th Sep. 1819.
Wheelock, L. P. ensign 31st	300.00	Advanced on account of bounties, &c.
Whitherbee, Samuel, lieutenant 31st	400.00	Advanced on account of bounties, &c.
Whistler, Jacob, ensign 16th	873.24	Balance on settlement, 20th July, 1820.

STATEMENT--Continued

Names and Rank	Amount Dolls.Cts.	Remarks
Williams, Alexander J. captain artillery	997.61	Balance on settlement, 26th November, 1819.
Ward, William, lieutenant 10th	266.96	Do do 8th July, 1818.
Winters, John, lieutenant	275.00	Advanced on account of quartermaster department.
Waters, David, lit. and quartermaster N.Y. militia	400.00	Advanced on account of quartermaster department.
Ward, Aaron, late lieutenant 29th	240.00	Balance on settlement 11th July, 1818.
Wilkinson, William, lieutenant 24th	300.00	Advanced on account of quartermaster department.
Wilkins, William W. paymaster militia	30,000.00	Reported for suit 22d July, 1818.
Wire, John, captain 30th	1,018.38	Account rendered without vouches for $960.38. He has rendered Other moneys not yet to his debit; making this balance.
West, P. lieutenant	391.10	Advanced on account of bounties and contingencies.
Walker, Elisha M. lieutenant 24th	548.00	Balance on settlement 24th August, 1818. Suspensions 286 rs.
Waring, John, lieutenant 14th	10.00	Do. do 3d September, 1818.
Worth, Barzillia, sea fencibles	8,409.68	Accounts rendered, and under examination.
Walker, John C. lieutenant 26th	1,459.36	Balance on settlement 5th August, 1816; $779.36. He is charged with 680 dollars, on account of bounties and contingencies; making this balance.
Williams, Byram, ensign 28th	266.00	Balance on settlement 22d September, 1818.
Warren, James, ensign 33d	155.79	Do do 1st January, 1820.
Wilson, Abiel, ensign 4th	196.75	Do do 6th October, 1818.
Webb, Stephen, lieutenant 30th	38.10	Do do 6th October, 1818.
Warley, Felix B. captain 8th	77.80	Do do 14th October, 1818.
Wimberly, Abner, paymaster 3d Georgia militia	1,490.96	Do do 16th October, 1820. Suspensions arising additional vouchers amounting to $60.98, and claims additional pay to that allowed $24.
Wiliams, John, ensign 3d riflemen	349.63	Balance on settlement 14th March, 1820.
Wilcox, Joseph M. lieutenant 3d infantry	301.43	Do do 6th November, 1818.
Williamson, John S. lieutenant 24th	431.34	Do do 15th February, 1819.
Woolly, Abraham R. major ordnance	295.00	Do do 19th March, 1819.
Wynkoop, James, J. lieutenant 29th	106.08	Do do 2d February, 1819.
White, Charles, sea fencibles	10,628.07	Accounts on file, and under examination.
Watkins, William, paymaster Kentucky militia	2,106.90	Balance on settlement, 8th March, 1819, and reported for suit October, 1820.
Wheeler, Francis T. lieutenant 13th	523.65	Do do 22d March, 1819. and reported for suit September, 1820.
Wood, Robert, late ensign 10th	451.00	Do do 25th March, 1819.

STATEMENT--Continued

Names and Rank	Amount Dolls.Cts.			Remarks
Witman, Charles, paymaster 1st Penn. Militia	36.80	Do	do	3d June, 1819.
Wagnon, Thomas P. lieutenant 28th	158.00	Do	do	22d April, 1819.
White, Benajah, lieutenant colonel 10th	4,605.50	Do	do	27th September, 1819.
Watkins, Gassaway, lieutenant 38th	542.00	Do	do	1st July, 1819.

STATEMENT--Continued

Names and Rank	Amount Dolls.Cts.	Remarks
Whitehead, A. lieutenant 5th	34.00	Balance on settlement 25th January, 1820.
Ward, James, assistant deputy quartermaster general	499.76	Do do 27th October, 1819.
Williams, Phineas, captain	1,235.00	Do do 30th October, 1819, and reported for suit 10th November, 1819.
Walkup, Samuel, paymaster 6th Va. militia	71.72	Do do 21st September, 1820.
Windle, Joseph H. assistant deputy paymaster	454,279.00	Accounts and vouchers rendered, and apparent balance of $10,965.90; further vouchers called for.
Whiting, Henry, captain 5th	20.00	Advanced on account of bounties, &c.
Watson, James J. paymaster	19.11	Balance on settlement 31st October, 1820. Suspensions to the full amount, which will be admissible on producing proper vouchers.
White, Clement, captain, 20th	XXX.12	Balance on settlement 30th June, 1815, $348.12. He has since refunded to the paymaster general $344, leaving this balance standing against him.
Wood, Christopher, captain, 26th	1X.85	Balance on settlement 9th September, 1819.
Wigging, Brungon B. quartermaster N. Y. militia ence to resoth October, 1819.	3,00X.95	Balance on settlement, 28th September, 1819, and reported for suit
West, Charles, ensign	19X.00	Advanced on account of bounties, &c.
Wellington, Henry, lieutenant 9th	17X.28	Balance on settlement 3d November, 1819.
Walthale, Henry, paymaster 5th Virginia militia	6,0XX.34	Do do 14th November, 1819.
Wheelock, Abel, lieutenant 2d dragoons	1XX.72	Do do 26th November, 1819.
Wilhight, Thomas C. lieutenant 18th	8XX.00	Accounts and vouchers rendered, upon which he claims 108 dollars, leaving an apparent balance of 710 dollars.
Williby, John, captain 27th	XXX.75	Balance on settlement 11th December, 1819.
Worster, Alexander, lieutenant 33d	XXX.51	Do do 21st December, 1819.
Wood, Josiah, captain 10th	1,9XX.00	Do do 4th December, 1819.
White, Philip, paymaster 3d Kentucky militia	2,0XX.08	Do do 10th October, 1819.
Wade, Nathan C. ensign 10th	2XX.00	Do do 24th January, 1820.
Young, Ignatius, F. lieutenant, 36th	4XX.00	Advanced on account of bounties, &c.
Young, James, lieutenant 6th	5XX.75	Balance on settlement 15th July, 1820.
Young, Robert, ensign 26th	1,XXX.00	Accounts and vouchers rendered, upon which he claims a balance due him.
Young, James M. lieutenant 30th	XX.00	Advanced on account of bounties and contingencies.
Yost, Philip, lieutenant 1st infantry	XX.00	Advanced on account of bounties and contingencies.

NOTE: This page had a major tear from top to bottom right through the Amount column. The X's were used according to spacing.

STATEMENT--Continued

Names and Rank	Amount Dolls.Cts.	Remarks
Yerby, Thomas, cornet Virginia militia	XX.00	Balance on settlement 29th August, 1820.
Yates, William C. ensign 5th	XX.40	Do do 24th April, 1816.
Young, Jonathan Y. lieutenant 30th	1XX.32	Advanced on account of bounties, &c.
Youngs, White, major 15th	407.51	Balance on settlement 20th October, 1817, $557.51. He is since credited with $150, leaving him indebted to the United States in the sum of $407.51; and reported for suit 26th September, 1814.
Yates, R. N. lieutenant 4th riflemen	XX.00	Advanced on account of bounties and contingencies.
Young, G. D. lieutenant colonel 29th	2,1XX.00	Advanced on account of bounties, &c.
Yelverton, Abijah, jun. paymaster N. Y. militia	7,XXX.58	Balance on settlement 28th June, 1820. Reported for suit.

NOTE: This page had a major tear from top to bottom right through the Amount column. The X's were used according to spacing.

Names and Rank	Amount Dolls.Cts.	Remarks
York, Jeremiah, lieutenant 31st	120.95	Balance on settlement 18th September, 1818.
Young, Thomas B. lieutenant 24th	124.00	Do do 4th December, 1818.
Young, Robert, paymaster 9th infantry	413.42	Do do 23d April, 1819.
Yale, Braddum, major N. Y. militia	125.00	Advanced on account of quartermaster department and militia.
Yancey, Lewis, lieutenant and paymaster 10th	4,817.36	Balance on settlement 11th December, 1819, and reported for suit 3d October, 1820.
Young, William, late lieutenant 7th	92.00	Do do 20th December, 1819.
Zantzinger, Richard A. lieutenant 2d artillery	20.20	Do do 12th February, 1819.

15,317.889.84

TREASURY DEPARTMENT,

THIRD AUDITOR'S OFFICE,

November 20, 1820.

No. 3

LIST of the names of Officers who have failed to render their accounts to the second Auditor of the Treasury, for settlement, within the last year, prior to the 30th September, 1820; exhibited in pursuance of the 13th section of the act of Congress, passed the 3d March, 1817, entitled "An act to provide for the prompt settlement of the public accounts.

NAMES.	RANK.	REMARKS.
James E. Denkins	brig. inspector	
Peter Leguex	ass.d.qr.m.gen.	
Wm. H. Hazard	hospt. Surgeon	
Lloyd Beall	late paymaster	Rept. To 1st Compt. Of Treasury for suit, 29th June, 1820.
J. Livingston	lieut. of ordn.	Do do 4th Feb. 1820.
G. D. Smith	brt. Maj. 2d inf.	Do do 3d May, 1820.
Samuel Brown	late dep. qr.m.g.	Do do 4th Feb. 1819.
John Sproul	brt.maj. 1st inf.	Do do 1st May, 1820.
Wm. McDonald	major	Do do 25th Oct. 1820.
John H. Mallory	late paymaster	Do do 4th Feb. 1820.
Daniel Brooks & Co.	contractors	Do do 24th Aug, 1819.
Stoughton Gantt	late paymaster	Do do 24th Aug. 1819.
Thos. Montgomery	late paymaster	Do do 15th Dec. 1818.
Robert M'Clallen	lieut. artillery	Do do 30th Sept. 1819.
William White	pension agent	Do do 28th Jan. 1820.
John Gates, junr.	late paymaster	Do do 12 Feb. 1818.
Peter Townsend	contractor	Do do 15th July, 1820.
Robert J. Scott	lieut. artillery	Do do 13th Dec. 1819.
White Youngs	brt. maj. infy.	Do do 6th Apr. 1820.
Alexander M'Rae	contractor	Do do 13th July, 1820.
Cornelius Gates	lieut. 8th infy.	Do do 15th Aug. 1820.
Peter Grayson	lieut. 3d infy.	Do do 8th June, 1820.
William Sumpter	capt. 1st infy.	Do do 15th Aug. 1820
Francis Smith	lieut. rif. regt.	Do do 8th June, 1820.
Peter Baudrey		Do do 15th July, 1820.
Harold Smith	captain	
Robert Lyman	lieutenant	
Thomas Martin	mil. store keep.	
Wm. T. Willard	lieut. artillery	
Willoughby Morgan	brt. major rif.	

LIST-Continued

NAMES.	RANK.	REMARKS.
F. S. Gray	lieut. 7th infy.	
F. L. Dade	lieut. 4th infy.	
Henry Leavenworth	lieut. colonel	
George Armistead	lt. col. Artillery	
77-10		
William Lawrence	lieut. colonel	
Joseph P. Prince	lieut. artillery	
Henry M. Simons,	lieut. artillery	
George W. Gardner	lieut. artillery	
Willis Foulk	capt. 8th infy.	
Moses Swett	capt. artillery	
Wm. D. Lawrence	late paymaster	
Charles Betts	lieut. 7th infy.	
Wm. S. Hamilton	lieut. col. rif. rg.	
Wm. Davenport	capt. 8th infy.	
Benjamin Birdsall	major rif. reg.	
J. Snelling,	lieut. colonel	
F. S. Amelung	capt. 1st infy.	
Joseph J. Miles	capt. 1st infy.	
John Tarrant	lieut. 1st infy.	
Gad. Humphreys	major 6th infy.	
J. P. Livingston	brevet captain	
Thomas M. Read	capt. 6th infy.	
Thomas G. Murray	capt. artillery	
Robert C. Nicholas	col. 8th infy.	
Kenneth M. Kenzie	capt. artillery	
John Biddle	capt. artillery	
P. R. Green	lieut. 5th infy.	
Wm. H. Nicholl	lieut. artillery	
Charles L. Cass	lieut. 3d infantry	
De La Fayette Wilcox	lieut. 6th infy.	
H. R. Dulany	lieut. 4th infy.	
Robert Searcey	act. paymaster	

LIST-Continued

NAMES.	RANK.	REMARKS.
James Reed	capt. artillery	
James Hackley	capt. 3d infy.	
C. M'Leod	lieut. 3d infy.	
A. Brownlow	capt. 8th infy.	
G. H. Kennerley	lieut. 8th infy.	
James C. Neilson		
John Page	lieut. 8th infy.	
W. Whatley	lieut. 8th infy.	
Luther Scott	captain	
James Palmer	lieut. 2d infy.	
Enos Cutler	major 2d infy.	
John Whitman	lieut. 8th infy.	
Nathaniel Young	lieut. 8th infy.	
Isaac E. Craig	lieut. artillery	
James S. Gray	captain rif. reg.	
Charles Harrison	lieut. 3d infy.	
John Ellison	lieut. 6th infy.	
Thomas S. Rogers	ass.dep.qr.m.g.	
James Pratt	capt. 5th infy.	
Barthw. Shaumburg	asst.paymaster	
Elijah Montgomery	captain	
R. B. Mason	lieut. 8th infy.	
J. Plympton	lieut. 5th infy.	
Joseph H. Rees	capt. ordnance	
Samuel Shannon	lieut. rif. reg.	
Farley Eddy	lieut. 8th infy.	
John J. H. Lewis	late lieut. rif. r.	
Loring Austin	major	
Ethan A. Hitchcock	lieut. 8th infy.	
J. B. Many	major rif. regt.	

LIST-Continued

NAMES.	RANK.	REMARKS.
Gabriel Field	lieut. rif. regt.	
E. W. Ripley	major general	
F. Le Griffith	lieut. artillery	
Q. B. Heronimus	lieut. 4th infy.	
Thomas J. Baird	lieut. &c.	
J. W. Thompson	lieut. ordnance	
John Gantt	lieut. rif. reg.	

TREASURY DEPARTMENT,

Second Auditor's Office, November 1st, 1820.

WM. LEE.

No. 4.

STATEMENT the Accounts of such Officers as have not rendered their Accounts within the year, or have Balances unaccounted for, advanced one year prior to the 30th September, 1819, as appears by the Books of the Third Auditor, furnished in pursuance of the directions of the First Comptroller of the Treasury, agreeably to the 13th section of the Act, passed 3d March, 1817, entitled "An Act to provide for the more prompt settlement of Public Accounts."

Names and Rank	Amount Dolls.Cts.	Remarks
Armistead, George, lieutenant colonel	7,150.94	Balance on settlement 29th January, 1820, for accounted rendered to 1818. Dead. His representatives promise an early settlement.
Armistead, Walker K. colonel	212.88	Balance on settlement 16th November, 1820.
Amelung, F. S. captain	192.88	Do do 24th March, 1819, for accounts rendered to 4th quarter, 1818.
Beall, Robert, lieutenant	2,237.98	Do do 3d May, 1819, for accounts rendered to 4th quarter, 1818, including 2000 dollars received 1st February, 1819.
Beauteau, Joab B. captain	30.00	No accounts rendered.
Chunn, John T. major	1,871.99	Amount of two drafts drawn by him for supplies furnished, the vouchers for which not being sufficient, the amount was charged to his personal account. The vouchers have not yet been perfected.
Coombes, Robert L. lieutenant	484.56	No accounts rendered.
Crupper, Micajah, captain	9,467.61	Balance on money advanced in 1817, per settlement 27th March, 1820. Accounts reported for suit 2d October, 1820.
Cobb, Waddy N. lieutenant	269.58	Balance on settlement 14th October, 1819, for accounts to 2d quarter, 1819.
Craig, Isaac E. lieutenant	20.00	No accounts rendered.
Curtis, Daniel, lieutenant	200.00	Ditto
Dorman, James, major	100.00	Ditto Dead.
Dinkins, James E. major	27.39	Balance on settlement 12th February, 1820, for accounts rendered to 1818.
Donoho, Sanders, captain	250.00	No accounts rendered.
Eveleth, Wm. S. lieutenant	846.82	Balance on settlement 22d August, 1818. Dead.
Easter, Richard I. captain	73,945.00	Has rendered accounts amounting to $31,583.22, which require explanation in part. He has been ordered to the seat of of government with the balance of his accounts for settlement, and is arrived for that purpose.

STATEMENT--Continued

Names and Rank	Amount Dolls.Cts.	Remarks
Fisher, Otis, lieutenant	12,107.77	Balance on settlement 21st June, 1819. Dead. His accounts will be Reported for suit.
Flourney, Alfred, major	100.00	No accounts rendered.
Foulk, Willis, captain	321.69	Ditto
Gratiot, Charles, major	2,808.38	Ditto. Balance on settlement 18th May, 1818. States that the balance will be refunded in a few days.
Gleason, Joseph, captain	136.66	Balance on settlement 20th October, 1819. of accounts rendered to 3d quarter, 1818. Dead.

Names and Rank	Amount Dolls.Cts.	Remarks
Gale, James H. lieutenant	342.44	Balance on settlement 24th March, 1819 for accounts rendered to 2d quarter 1818.
Gray, Robert, major	50.00	No accounts rendered.
Gantt, Stoughton, captain	375.80	Balance on settlement, 4th December, 1819, of accounts rendered for 1814.
Gray, James S. lieutenant	110.00	No accounts rendered.
Gannt, John, lieutenant	204.73	Ditto
Grosvenor, George H. captain	63.00	Ditto
Gaines, E. P. general	2,755.38	Balance on settlement 13th November, 1820.
Humphreys, E. major	107.74	Do do 1st September, 1819.
Heard, Franklin C. major of Georgia militia	6,000.00	Advanced on account of provisions for the Georgia troops in 1818. No accounts rendered.
Heard, Morgan A. captain of Tennessee militia	41.31	Balance on settlement 28th September, 1820, for accounts rendered to 2d quarter 1818.
Hart, R. W. colonel of Tennessee militia	50.00	No accounts rendered.
Irvine, Robert, lieutenant	100.00	Ditto
Kirby, Robert M. major	122.00	Ditto
Kieser, Christopher, captain	10,399.35	Balance on settlement 27th February, 1820. This money was advanced to pay off accounts for which he had become personally responsible. His death, which happened shortly after, it is presumed, prevented the transmission of receipts. The payments, it is believe, have been made.
Lyman, Robert, lieutenant	7,047.03	Accounts settled 3d September, 1818. None since rendered.
Lawshe, Lewis, lieutenant	14.88	Balance on settlement 29th September, 1818.
Leavenworth, Henry, colonel	192.17	Accounts rendered to 3d quarter 1819, amounting to $41.38, and returned to him for explanation. His distance, doubtless, prevented the transmission of other accounts in time.
M'Donald, Wm. major	401.32	No accounts rendered. Out of service. Will be reported for suit.
Maul, John P. lieutenant	1,104.27	Balance on settlement, 7th July, 1819, for accounts rendered to 4th quarter 1818. Has suspended vouchers, which he says requires time to perfect.
Melvin, George. W. Captain	1,022.99	Balance on settlement, 13th May, 1820, for accounts to 4th quarter 1817.
Martin, Wyley, captain	500.40	Do do 3d September, 1819.
M'Clintock, William, lieutenant	57.63	Do do 23d December, 1818.
Miller, James, general	86.81	Do do 18th May, 1818.

STATEMENT--Continued

Names and Rank	Amount Dolls.Cts.	Remarks
M'Cabe, Robert, lieutenant	242.54	Do do 15th May, 1820, for accounts rendered in 1819.
Nelson, Joseph S. captain	150.00	No accounts rendered.
Prince, Joseph P. lieutenant	800.00	Ditto
Pratt, James, captain	1,050.00	Ditto
Payne, M. M. captain	123.22	Balance on settlement 16th May, 1818.
Passons, Thomas, lieutenant	40.00	No accounts rendered.
Pickett, James C. assistant deputy quartermaster gen.	2,941.00	Balance on settlement 22d November, 1819, for accounts rendered to 3d quarter 1819. Confined by sickness. Promises immediately to render his accounts.
Perry, David, captain	1,173.66	No accounts rendered.

STATEMENT--Continued

Names and Rank	Amount Dolls.Cts.	Remarks
Parkhurst, J. lieutenant	100.00	No accounts rendered.
Poussin, William T. captain	124.00	Ditto
Russey, R. E. De. Captain	398.27	Balance on settlement 9th March, 1819.
Romayne, James T. B. captain	400.00	No accounts rendered.
Roberson, William L. captain	2,797.67	Balance on settlement 16th October, 1819. Out of service. Will settle his accounts.
Riddle, David, major	4,761.75	No accounts rendered. Dead.
Ripley, E. W. general	4,057.93	Ditto do Reported for suit 2d October, 1820.
Rogers, Thomas S. captain	14,544.63	Balance on settlement 8th October, 1819. Dead. His accounts will be forwarded by his administrator.
Smith, John L. lieutenant	384.00	Balance on settlement 22d October, 1819.
Swift, Joseph G. general	3,104.05	Accounts rendered 16th November, 1820, on which this balance Appears.
Shell, Henry, captain	50.00	No accounts rendered.
Sumpter, William, lieutenant	300.00	Ditto
Sands, A. L. lieutenant	71.79	Balance on settlement, 9th August, 1819.
Smith, G. D. lieutenant	121.59	Balance on settlement, 27th April, 1818.
Stockton, Thomas, major	200.00	No accounts rendered.
Shannon, Samuel, lieutenant	27.00	Balance on settlement 21st April, 1820, for accounts rendered to 3d quarter 1819.
Stubbs, James R. captain	150.00	No accounts rendered.
Totten, Joseph G. lieutenant colonel	1,635.82	Apparent balance of accounts rendered to include 2d quarter 1819.
Tarrant, John, lieutenant	1,729.00	No accounts rendered.
Taylor, John P. lieutenant	51.40	Balance on settlement, 6th July, 1818.
Thomas, Martin, lieutenant	40.00	No accounts rendered.
West, George, major	50.00	Ditto
Willis, Lewis B. captain	41.83	Balance on settlement, 9th August, 1819.
Worth, William J. major	206.23	Do do 29th October, 1819.
Washburn, Samuel, lieutenant	742.30	Do do 26th September, 1820, for accounts rendered to 3d quarter 1819, arising from suspensions or disallowances.

STATEMENT--Continued

Names and Rank	Amount Dolls.Cts.	Remarks
Wilkin, G. S. lieutenant	50.00	No accounts rendered.
Wood, John, lieutenant	364.87	Balance on settlement 28th March, 1820, for accounts to 3d Quarter 1819.

TREASURY DEPARTMENT,

THIRD AUDITOR'S OFFICE,

November 17, 1820.

PETER HAGNER, *Auditor*

No. 5

ABSTRACT of Moneys advanced prior to the 3d of March, 1809, on the books of the late Accountant of the War Department, and which remained to be accounted for on the books of the third Auditor of the Treasury, on the 30th of September, 1820.

Names and Rank	Amount Dolls.Cts.	Remarks
Armstrong, John, late captain	10.36	Dead. No accounts rendered.
Armistead, John B. late captain	100.00	On account of his pay.
Armstrong, Hamilton	56.00	
Allen, Hannibal M. late lieutenant	15.21	Overpaid on his subsistence account.
Armistead, Walker K.	26.00	Balance on settlement.
Armistead, A. B. captain	48.00	Advanced for recruiting.
Atkinson, Henry, colonel	252.82	Balance on settlement.
Blake, Philemon, C. late lieutenant	4.00	Balance on settlement.
Blount, Jacob, late contractor for gun carriages	750.00	On account of his contract.
Bludworth, James, late lieutenant	68.88	Balance on settlement.
Bam, William C. late captain	486.00	Balance on settlement. Dead.
Bowie, James G. late captain	600.00	On account of recruiting.
Bankhead, James, major	328.74	Balance on settlement.
Bird, Ross, late captain	151.63	Balance on settlement.
Brook, George M. colonel	150.00	Advanced for recruiting.
Beesly, Maurice, late captain Pennsylvania militia	873.02	For pay of the militia, in 1794. The money was advanced on certified rolls, and ascertained to be due, but the receipts have not been produced.
Coosman, Andrew, late paymaster New Jersey militia	19,195.82	do. do. do.
Clark, James, late captain Pennsylvania militia	699.83	do. do. do.
Chandler, Richard, late paymaster	8,204.42	Balance on settlement. Dead and insolvent.
Clarke, John, late major levies	11.08	Balance on settlement.
Cumming, John, late lieutenant	255.11	Balance on settlement 27th June, 1802.
Campbell, Joseph, late lieutenant	43.20	Overdrawn on his subsistence account.
Clarke, Cary, late lieutenant	32.32	Overdrawn on his subsistence account.
Claiborne, Ferdinand L. brigadier general volunteers	500.00	Accounts rendered, but imperfect.
Clements, Thomas, late lieutenant	6.06	Balance on settlement.
Cross, Joseph, late lieutenant	88.72	Balance on settlement.
Cross, Ebenezer, late captain	204.60	Balance on settlement.
Cherry, Samuel, late captain	2,144.04	Advanced for recruiting and contingent expenses. Dead and insolvent.

STATEMENT--Continued

Names and Rank	Amount Dolls.Cts.	Remarks
Constant, Joseph, lieutenant colonel	224.90	For pay.
Carson, William, late lieutenant, &c.	278.00	Advanced him in 1810.
Carter, John C. late ensign	109.67	Balance on settlement. Dead.
Cashman, Alden G. late lieutenant	36.00	On account of recruiting.
Chambers, James, late lieutenant and paymaster	471.88	Balance on settlement. Dead.
Crocker, Dodridge, late cor.	163.34	
Davis, Thomas, late captain	20.00	Balance on settlement, 22d November, 1812.
Doyle, Thomas, late captain militia	91.57	Balance on settlement. Dead.
Daniel, Cordial N. late surgeons mate	45.75	Balance on settlement.
Duforist, John V. late ensign	8.60	Balance on settlement.
Doane, Josiah, late captain	35.73	Balance on settlement.
Dorman, James, lieutenant	50.00	On account recruiting.
Dale, Richard, late captain	21.41	Balance on settlement.
Dunham, James, late major militia	2,432.94	For pay of the militia, in 1794. The amount advanced on rolls and ascertained to be due, but the receipts have not been produced.
Dayton, William, late paymaster New Jersey militia	12,021.06	Balance of his account for paying militia on the western expedition of 1794. Has other claims.
Duffield, Edward, late paymaster Pennsylvania militia	10,576.92	For pay of militia in 1794. The amount advanced on rolls and ascertained to be due, but the receipts have never been produced.
Evans, Walter, late paymaster militia	7,388.64	do. do. do.
Eddy, George, late paymaster militia	6,949.13	do. do. do.
Elder, Thomas, late paymaster militia	2,211.15	do. do. do.
Everitt, Samuel, late major militia	2,105.21	do. do. do.
Eastman, Jonathan, late lieutenant, &c.	91.32	For amount of stoppage against captain Archibald Danah.
Emery, Ephraim, late lieutenant	120.12	Balance on settlement.
Easterbrook, Nathan, late captain	164.42	Balance on settlement.
Edmonds, Elias, lieutenant	500.00	On account of recruiting.
Eustis, Abraham, major	1,886.39	On account of recruiting.
Fergus, John, late lieutenant	39.72	Balance on settlement.
Findley, David, late captain	179.43	Balance on settlement. Dead.
Findley, Ebenezer, late paymaster militia	2,686.30	For pay of the militia in 1794. The amount advanced on rolls, and ascertained to be due, but no accounts have been produced.
Foster, Thomas, late lieutenant colonel militia	6,086.46	Do. do. do.

STATEMENT--Continued

Names and Rank	Amount Dolls.Cts.	Remarks		
Fisher, George, late major militia	1,221.66	Do.	do.	do.
Greer, John, late paymaster militia	2,791.96	Do.	do.	do.
Glasco, John, late contractor	300.00	He has furnished timber at Greenleaf's Point, but no accounts have been rendered.		
Gratiot, Charles, lieutenant colonel	100.00	On account of pay, &c.		

STATEMENT--Continued

Names and Rank	Amount Dolls.Cts.	Remarks
Hughes, Thomas, late captain	31.36	Balance on settlement.
Hukile, Levi, cornet	1,519.44	Dead
Horton, John, lieutenant	18.00	Balance on settlement.
Hutchins, William, captain	19.48	Balance on settlement.
Houtson, Mossman, captain	668.50	Balance on settlement.
Harvey, Benjamin, ensign	50.00	On account of recruiting.
Hook, Moses, captain	12,163.91	Balance on settlement, 2d October, 1815. Reported for suit.
Hannah, James, colonel militia	6,050.25	For pay of militia in 1794. This money was advanced on rolls, and ascertained to be due, but no receipts have been produced.
Henderson, William, late captain militia	243.03	Do. do. do.
Harris, William, late paymaster militia	9,544.37	Do. do. do.
Hubbard, Thomas, captain militia	540.82	Do. do. do.
Johnston, Francis, captain militia	172.99	Balance on settlement. Dead.
Jackson, Jacob, late lieutenant	24.53	Overpaid on his pay and subsistence accounts by the paymaster.
Irvine, Willian N. late captain	330.49	Balance on settlement, 8th July, 1811.
Johnston, William, lieutenant	42.00	Do. do. 9th July, 1812.
Kalteisen, Michael, captain	123.40	Do. do. do.
Kimball, Joseph, lieutenant	1,624.30	Balance of money placed in his hands by the military agent.
Kinglsey, Alpha, lieutenant	20.00	Advanced for different purposes. No accounts rendered.
Lewis, Samuel, sen. late clerk in War Office	2,565.55	Balance remaining in his hands.
Landais, Lewis, late lieutenant	56.00	Advanced in 1803, for recruiting.
Leybourn, John do	141.50	Balance on settlement, 14th May, 1807
Lee, Thomas, do	612.00	Accounts rendered and sworn to, but no vouchers, and could not therefore be settled.
Logan, James, late ensign	353.45	Advanced for recruiting, &c.
Law, Prentis, captain	146.00	Balance on settlement, 20th May, 1811. Dead.
Laval, Jacent, colonel	135.57	Balance on settlement.
Lomax, Edward L. ensign	200.00	Advanced for recruiting. Dead.
Lithgow, William M. lieutenant	65.25	Balance on settlement, 4th May, 1810. Dead.
Lee, William A. captain	500.00	
Lamkin, Peter, lieutenant	208.00	Balance on settlement
Lee, Washington, do.	186.18	Do. do.
Lawrence, Thomas, late paymaster militia	7,795.69	Advanced for pay of the militia in 1794. This money was advanced on roles, and ascertained to be due; but the receipts not produced.

STATEMENT--Continued

Names and Rank	Amount Dolls.Cts.	Remarks		
Light, John, late major militia	1,835.10	Do.	do.	do.
Marsh, Joseph, late paymaster militia	3,045.60	Do	do.	do.
M'Dermot, Paul, do do	11,641.72	Do.	do.	do.

Names and Rank	Amount Dolls.Cts.	Remarks
May, Daniel, colonel militia	4,789.05	Advanced for pay of militia in 1794. The money was advanced on on rolls, and ascertained to be due, but the vouchers not produced.
Mosher, Jeremiah, colonel militia	4,425.53	Do. do. do.
M'Mickle, John, late ensign	20.00	Dead; no account rendered.
Miller, William, do	70.11	No accounts rendered.
Mead, William C. do	196.50	
M'Guire, Samuel, late lieutenant	145.09	On account recruiting.
Magnan, Charles, ensign	41.00	Overpaid, on his pay and subsistence account, by the paymaster.
Millikin, John , express	100.00	On account of his services and expenses as an express.
Melvin, George W. captain	110.08	
Mecklenburg, Peter, major	136.75	Balance on settlement
Marsh, Samuel	118.23	Ditto
Noland, Enos, late lieutenant	35.00	Ditto
Newman, Francis do	12.79	Overpayment for transportation.
Osborne, Robert W. do	158.00	Balance of money placed in his hands as assistant military agent.
Oldham, Richard	124.62	Advanced for recruiting.
Opie, Le Roy	205.82	Balance on settlement.
Pendergrast, Garret, late surgeon's mate	3.60	Overpaid on his subsistence account, by the paymaster.
Prior, Abner, late captain	41.52	Balance on settlement. Dead.
Powell, John F. do	10.65	Balance on settlement.
Phillips, Henry, late lieutenant	389.00	Ditto
Pemberton, John, late ensign	2.50	Ditto
Prescott, George W. late captain	130.14	Advanced by military agent, by order of General Wilkinson.
Price, Samuel, late lieutenant	881.00	Advanced by the paymaster, in 1808.
Purdy, Robert, colonel	200.00	Advanced for recruiting.
Rand, Benjamin, late ensign	150.00	
Read, James, late captain	160.00	Advanced for recruiting.
Rinnick, Seymour, late lieutenant	248.00	Balance on settlement.
Ridgeway, Fielder, captain	68.40	Advanced for recruiting..
Ragan, John do	187.82	Balance on settlement
Roney, John, late lieutenant	232.00	Ditto
Roney, John, late lieutenant	500.00	Advanced for recruiting
Rathbun, S. B. late lieutenant	18.60	Balance on settlement
Rose, Alexander	105.32	Ditto

STATEMENT--Continued

Names and Rank	Amount Dolls.Cts.	Remarks
Robinson, Thomas, paymaster	7,625.32	Advanced for pay of militia in 1794. No receipt produced.

STATEMENT--Continued

Names and Rank	Amount Dolls.Cts.	Remarks
Salmon, George paymaster	22,787.85	
Stewart, Daniel do	3,917.16	
Stephenson, Stephen, lieutenant colonel militia	1,402.81	
Sevier, Jon, brigadier general	1,602.73	
Saxon, John, lieutenant	121.00	
Symes, John C. ensign	38.91	
Sparkhawk, Jonathan H.	1.16	
Smith, James S. lieutenant	1,803.55	
Sebastian, Alfred, do	300.00	
Scott, Winfield, major general	509.54	
Sufferers of the Connecticut Land Company	932.12	
Strode, Thomas, late captain	900.28	
Steward, Benedict, lieutenant	120.00	
Sparks, Richard, major	540.80	
Smith, John, colonel	1.00	
Sumpter, Thomas	50.00	
Thompson, Robert, late lieutenant	170.00	
Toomy, John, sergeant major	5.41	
Thompson, John W. ensign	16.87	
Taylor, Charles M. lieutenant	39.00	
Townsend, Solomon D. captain	447.65	
Taylor, Edward, late captain militia	801.70	
Woodruff, Abner, late paymaster militia	16,731.87	
Wharton, Karney, paymaster militia	15,971.14	
Whitney, Moses, captain	846.13	
Woodruff, Joseph, captain	55.26	
Williams, Robert, governor Mississippi territory	1,974.81	
Williams, Leonard, late lieutenant	211.17	

NOTE: REMARKS PORTION OF TORN PAGE DO NOT LINE UP WITH THE NUMBERS, SO REMARKS HAVE
BEEN EXCLUDED FOR THIS PAGE.

Names and Rank	Amount Dolls.Cts.	Remarks
Waterhouse, George, captain	260.20	Balance on settlement. Dead
Wooldridge, William H.	140.00	Being the amount of his note given to Thomas A. Smith, then a Lieutenant of artillery, for a public horse.
Wilkins, John, jun. late quartermaster general	70,970.54	By accounts rendered, a balance is claimed; but large deductions and Suspensions were made by the accountant, not since removed.
Ware, William F. ensign	4.50	Balance on settlement.
Webster, Rezin, captain militia	256.09	
Walton, Benjamin, captain	756.1X	Arising out of moneys advanced for recruiting and contingencies.
Wilkinson, James, major general	5,627.03	Balance on settlement 9th October, 1819.
	313,617.XX	

X used for missing numbers

TREASURY DEPARTMENT,

THIRD AUDITOR'S OFFICE,

November, 21, 1820

PETER HAGNER, *Auditor*

Montgomery County, Tennessee 1850 Agricultural Census

New Madrid County, Missouri Marriage Records, 1899–1924

North Carolina 1850 Agricultural Census: Volumes 1–4

Pemiscot County, Missouri Marriage Records, January 26, 1898 to September 20, 1912: Volume 1

Pemiscot County, Missouri Marriage Records, November 1, 1911 to December 6, 1922: Volume 2

South Carolina 1860 Agricultural Census: Volumes 1–3

Tennessee 1850 Agricultural Census: Volumes 1–5

Tennessee 1860 Agricultural Census: Volumes 1 and 2

Texas 1850 Agricultural Census, Volume 1: Anderson through Hunt Counties

Texas 1850 Agricultural Census, Volume 2: Jackson through Williamson Counties

Texas 1860 Agricultural Census, Volumes 1–5

Virginia 1850 Agricultural Census, Volumes 1–5

Virginia 1860 Agricultural Census, Volumes 1–4

West Virginia 1850 Agricultural Census, Volumes 1 and 2

West Virginia 1860 Agricultural Census, Volume 1–4

www.ingramcontent.com/pod-product-compliance
Lightning Source LLC
Chambersburg PA
CBHW080613270326
41928CB00016B/3034